TOTAL *Intimacy*

A Guide to Loving by Color

Douglas Rosenau, Ed.D.
Deborah Neel, Ph.D.

Sexual
Wholeness
RESOURCES

SexualWholeness.com
Atlanta, GA

Paperback ISBN: 978-0-9858107-2-6

ePub ISBN: 978-0-9858107-3-3

Front cover by Josh Feit, Evangela.com

Drawings by Michael Dolan, Dolanadvertising.com

To Catherine Rosenau & John Neel,
our valued partners through these many years,
you bring such organization, meaning
and total intimacy
to our lives and marriages.

And

To you brave and faithful readers
who seek to imitate our transforming Redeemer,
may your love experience deeper and richer hues
and your marriages overflow
with that synergizing love and joy of
Total Intimacy.

"Two are better than one,
A cord of three strands is not quickly broken."

Ecclesiastes 4:9a, 12b

TABLE OF CONTENTS

INTRODUCTION

*And this is my prayer: that your love may abound more and
more in knowledge and depth of insight.*

Philippians 1:9

God created each of us to be loved. We want to be considered
special, to be treasured for our unique personality, quirks and
appeal. We long to be in an intimate relationship with someone,
especially a mate, who will *pursue us, fully know, love and accept us.*
Our spouses desire the same.

This mutual love and commitment, to know that we matter,
that we are chosen, builds trust and the foundation for a pulsating
physical chemistry. Lovers want to feel in love as they revel in an
amazing sexual passion "until death do us part." Yes! We want to, and
can, make love for a lifetime, even into our seventies and eighties.

What an exciting privilege it is to marry and become Covenant
Lovers[1] with another person! When we say, "I do," we are making
an everlasting promise, a covenant, *to* one another *before* God. It
is a lifetime commitment of fidelity and of pursuing relational and

sexual oneness. As Covenant Lovers, *the seal or symbol of our covenant is sexual lovemaking.* The loving creative Trinity desires every marriage to have a great sex life.

At least four times in scripture God makes this foundational statement: *"For this reason a man will leave his father and mother and be united to his wife and the two will become one flesh..."* (Genesis 2:24-25, Matthew 19:5, Mark 10:7-8, Ephesians 5:31-32).

This marital oneness is not a command to sameness but rather a choice to mutually partner with and fulfill one another. It is two whole people choosing to enter into an emotional and physical union that is romantically sexual. Sexual intercourse powerfully symbolizes the bonding of "becoming one flesh." Too often we forget that this one-flesh relationship goes deeper than physical intimacy. It is a whole spectrum of foundational relationship "adhesives" that bond and energize a 3-dimensional (body, mind with emotions, and heart) sexual connecting.

Total Intimacy Defined

What does the concept of total intimacy conjure up in your mind? Maybe you see it as an arrogant claim or a teasing idea that can never really be achieved. Or, perhaps you are more hopeful and the words stimulate a longing for something new, different and fulfilling—*a love that can transform your marriage!*

We use the word "total" to express the concept of a *balanced, complete intimacy* with all the necessary ingredients. Just as a healthy diet nourishes us with a broad spectrum of foods containing all the important vitamins and nutrients, total intimacy nourishes deeper growth and connection in marriage. Total does not imply that perfection has been reached or even that perfection is the ultimate goal you must strive to achieve.

A pediatrician once advised the parents of a picky eater, "Don't worry if every meal has the perfect combination from the food chart; just aim for providing the foods over a week's time and your child will have balanced nutrition." Total intimacy is wisely combining different types of intimacy over the days, weeks and months. This will help us experience a richer, more passionate love-making through the years.

...so that you may be mature and complete, not lacking anything.
James 1:4

"Intimacy" describes a special kind of familiarity, with a love and understanding that continues to grow. Although we may experience it as physical attraction or chemistry, it is motivated by a desire to really know another person and allow that person to experientially know us. Intimacy is sharing our feelings and our lives with our partner. Over time, we develop trust as we treat one another (and are treated) with total honesty, kindness, empathy and acceptance. This is the foundation for a growing physical and emotional attachment.

The intensity or depth of the relationship will increase as a meaningful shared history develops. When a relationship turns romantic, we begin to view one another as "us," not just "I" or "me". We want to spend more time together, serve one another and share more of ourselves. This mix of emotional and physical intimacy powerfully interlaces and creates a vibrant connection.

Total intimacy is a feeling of *comprehensive and abundant* closeness that bonds us; it is what we long for in marriage. In a totally intimate marriage, we share feelings, thoughts, hopes, dreams, attitudes, behaviors, and bodies with acceptance and without fear or criticism. Total Intimacy's warm embrace is the opposite of cold, distant loneliness—or two bored and resentful spouses who feel like roommates.

Total Intimacy is not for the faint-hearted! But the payoff is *life-changing*.

In marriage, emotional and sexual intimacy is intertwined and complementary. When they are well developed and integrated, they generate a dynamic bonding between two people that reflects God's relationship with us and the "oneness" of the Trinity. In this relationship, we exemplify *love* like our Creator loves.

Culture tends to define sex in terms of bodies and performance. But Total Intimacy is deeper than body involvement; it includes our hearts and our minds with our emotions. Sex is not "just sex" but a shared love. It is passion, closeness, renewed energy and connection. How fascinating is God's incredible creation that through our bodies and erogenous zones we can convey our heartfelt feelings and bond with our lover in awe-inspiring ways.

Total Intimacy, complete and vulnerable openness, encourages us to play, communicate, joyfully anticipate, laugh and surrender to one another—with our hearts and bodies passionately alive. It replicates Adam and Eve in the Garden who were physically and emotionally "naked and unashamed." This relationship model is not easily achieved, but the payoff is life-changing!

There is no fear in love. But, perfect love drives out fear...
I John 4:18

Total Intimacy does not automatically occur in a marriage. Without careful attention, it may never develop and it can quickly disappear. It is difficult, if not impossible, to "make love" to a spouse that you do not like or trust—nor is this what God intends for us. God earnestly desires for us to feel "in love" when we "make love." In order to do so *we need to understand all that "in love" includes.*

We encourage you to embark on a journey that explores this model of Covenant Lovers who share *Total Intimacy* and know what it means to really be "in love." If you put this into practice, it will lead you into a deeper and more exciting marriage and sex life.

Couples will read this book for a variety of reasons. Some are trying to rebuild intimacy after the trauma of sexual abuse or infidelity. Others want to reignite a sex life grown stale or routine, or one that never quite equaled their hopes and dreams. Many couples want to experience "more" and add those sparks that can enrich their already satisfying lovemaking.

We also intend for this book to help women find their sexual voice. We are saddened by the number of Christian wives who don't enjoy sex for themselves, but see it as a service they provide for their husbands. I Corinthians 7:3-5 makes it very clear that sexual fulfillment becomes a *mutual* responsibility and privilege in a good marriage. Husbands and wives should be reciprocally experiencing sexual pleasure and contentment.

Covenant Lovers in pursuit of Total Intimacy must work to build and maintain three categories of intimacy to enjoy one-flesh passion and a transforming love. The three types of intimacy are: Bonding, Coupling and Igniting. Each type is represented here by a color, and each one is practiced in all 3-dimensions: body, mind with emotions, and heart. In Christian dating relationships, the colors and intimacy develop sequentially. In marriage, all three colors, beautifully and intentionally practiced as balanced nutrition, contribute to the "total" we crave and to a picture of marital love that is reflective of God's design.

Our hope is that *Total Intimacy: A Guide to Loving by Color* will help you appreciate and define your needs as intimate companions and erotic playmates, and that you will integrate these concepts and practices into your marriage. We pray that with God's help, you will find hope, healing and passion.

I came that they might have life, and have it abundantly.
John 10:10b (NASB)

Note: The heart of this book is in the discussion questions at the end of each section. They will help you apply these lessons to your own love relationship. Take time to carefully consider each question and apply the insights you have gained, as you *practice* engaging in Total Intimacy.

With years of experience as marital and sex therapists, we cannot overemphasize the importance of dialogue and discussion for intimate relationships and a great sex life. Read sections of Total Intimacy out loud to each other; create conversations about your lovemaking; heal those old wounds; use the questions to drive you deeper. Learning to talk comfortably with your spouse about your love life will bring amazing results.

IN LOVING COLOR

The colors of intimacy are broad categories of connecting with and expressing love to our marriage partner. Each color represents an important aspect of intimacy that is built and sustained with distinct, vital practices. Personality, family background, past sexual experiences, and gender all influence how we understand and practice the colors. The colors may come more naturally to some people than to others. But, take heart! *The behaviors and attitudes encouraged by each color can be learned.*

If the habit of practicing the colors is never learned, neglected or their importance forgotten (just like healthy eating)—your marital health will suffer. Our therapy hours are full of couples who are in this tragic, heartbreaking place. Thank you for reading this book and focusing on the godly, healthy maintenance of your love relationship.

The colors of Total Intimacy create synergy! Each color contributes uniquely to your marriage, and the interaction of colors produces an invigorating effect far greater than any one color alone. The more fully we incorporate and practice them with our spouse, the deeper and more satisfying the intimacy and relationship we will have.

The Colors

GREEN   Intimate Companions (Bonding)
PURPLE Sensuous Lovers   (Coupling)
ORANGE Erotic Playmates   (Igniting)

As a memory aid, we chose a specific color to best represent each category of intimacy. Just as each of these colors are created by the joining of two primary colors, it will take both husband and wife to create each color in their relationship. All three colors exist in a *continuum* of shades: light chartreuse to deep forest green; lavender to deep purple; peach or tangerine to a deep burnt orange. The deeper the color's shade, the greater the intimate connection becomes.

Green is the fundamental color of life in nature. It brings to mind leaves and photosynthesis, the biological process that keeps all of creation alive. In relationships, Green represents the foundational element of simple companionship. Green intimacy includes the characteristics of special and significant friendships, such as relationships with family members, a close "bud" and the friend you've had since high school. Romantic couples tend to move toward the more vulnerable closeness reflected in the darker shades of Green.

In marriage, the solid Green foundation of liking your spouse and being friends extends beyond the depths of other friendships to a bonding, trusting, uninhibited transparency. This sets the stage for deeper intimacy and awesome lovemaking. Green intimacy is required before authentic Purple and Orange intimacy can be experienced.

Purple is the rich and sensuous color of royalty. It is the color most often associated with kings and queens who don purple robes to display their wealth and majesty. We emphasize the vital importance of purple intimacy by giving it this magnificent color.

Purple includes romantic flirtation, sexual attraction and coupling—becoming an exclusive "item." Purple behaviors only take place between committed lovers; it is characterized by deep kissing, extended cuddling, long hugs, playful flirtation and sensuous touches. Dating couples remain in lighter shades of the Purple spectrum.

Purple intimacy can be described as: soulfully enticing, enthusiastically uninhibited, focused sensuality, and sexually exciting. Purple may trigger erotic arousal but its goal is not sexual completion—so boundaries are set with a commitment to discipline physical responses. *Purple intimacy doesn't lead to something else; it is being fully experientially present.* It is not intended to be foreplay and to automatically result in Orange behaviors. The intent of Purple sexual intimacy is flirtatiousness and sensuous engagement with your partner to enhance being "in love" and intimate coupling.

This category, Purple, is the one most often neglected in marriage. Wives, and many husbands, yearn for it. Purple behaviors are most responsible for keeping the two of you *lovers* and not just roommates.

The color ***Orange*** is startling, like a fire that is being lit. Artists and gardeners use orange in their palate intentionally, and usually sparingly, for its ability to attract and hold attention. The hot visual power of orange exceeds the heat of the common Valentine's red.

Orange intimacy encompasses the intense emotional and physical connections that God designed for marriage and only for marriage. This degree of intimacy combines feelings of powerful transcending closeness with the pursuit of sexual arousal and satisfaction between erotic playmates. It employs the full range of possibilities in lovemaking: comfortable connection with enjoyable foreplay, extended stretches of heightened fun, quickies for a jolt of pleasure, and amazing volcanoes of multiple orgasms.

We hope that our color-coding system makes Total Intimacy

easy to remember for helpful application within your marriage. We encourage you to have fun with the colors and use them as shorthand to communicate the type of intimacy you need at a given time: "Oh wow, the *purple* flower is on her pillow. She wants nurturing, sensuous touch but she may not have the energy for more than that. I will follow her lead if she changes her mind."

Remember, the colors are a continuum from light to dark, and the darker shades convey deeper relational intensity. They can blend and blur together—when dark green cuddling becomes a light purple lover's embrace. Deep purple showering together can convert into the light orange of foreplay. But, as we define each color you will see it that has its own unique purpose and goal.

As you begin to understand and apply the three colors of intimacy, take the time to experience them fully. Remember that God created us as 3-dimensional lovers. We have a body with sexual desires, arms and legs to wrap around each other and the wonderful ability to express affection through touches and kisses.

If there are Wounds...

and you are recovering from past or present sexual distress of an affair, sexual dysfunction or trauma, you may initially need to avoid Orange and focus on the lighter shades of Green and Purple intimacy. Move towards the darker shades, as you are able; the deeper hues may be more anxiety-provoking. If there is past trauma, caution must be taken to avoid triggering bad memories and re-traumatizing. Allow a slow pace as you strategically build the foundational intimacy necessary before surrendering to full sexual arousal. Accept where you are. With a peaceful attitude of love and forgiveness, stretch yourself towards God's design for you. You CAN get there. This book is a starting point but do not hesitate to seek professional help to assist you in your healing journey.

We have a mind that includes an amygdala, our emotional feeling center, and a prefrontal cortex for making wise decisions. And, we have hearts that hunger to feel completed—to be chosen by a special person as a lover. Our desire is for you as a couple to experience love in all three dimensions in new and transformative ways.

Appreciate and embrace the Discussion Questions; they will help you *apply the colors*. Remember, these questions are the heart of this book and the path to revolutionizing your marital intimacy.

Before you work through the book, stop a minute to think through and discuss with your mate what patterns and behaviors have sabotaged your past endeavors to improve your marriage. Too busy? Wounds? Old resentments? A lack of trust? Not prioritizing and being intentional? Let's make it different this time around.

We commend you for taking the time to be courageous and intentionally disciplined. Allow the questions to inspire change. Our prayer for your marriage is that you can enjoy the rich rewards of learning to love by color.

Green
INTIMATE COMPANIONS

Bonding Intimacy

Green intimacy, like the grass and trees in nature, emphasizes the living and ever-growing connection of *authentic friendships*. Green "Intimate Companions" can include the closeness of male and female friendships and the warm fellowship of a family or community. Green is also the bedrock of that special companionship of marriage.

Just as photosynthesis in green grass fosters its growth, in marriage, Green intimacy nurtures the growth of a *bonded* lover-companionship. Covenant Lovers are best friends and the things that we do to develop and maintain lover-friends are the same things that we do to build positive, long-lasting friendships with our children, friends, siblings, parents and others. Though the Green in marriage remains unique, it is not intended to be erotic; it too is meant to be *bonding*.

Green intimacy keeps a married couple feeling 'in like' and helps couples fall back in love with each other. How many times have you heard people say, "I love him (or her); I just don't like him right now"? Tragically, the fun and the bonding activities that sustain intimate companionships are often replaced in marriage with 'being responsible' and family management, which often leaves spouses feeling like roommates or business partners.

A mutual, bonding friendship is foundational to marriage and cultivates true partnering. Bonding requires that mates learn to share their feelings, build effective communication practices, and trust and esteem one another. They must also engage in connecting behaviors, enjoying ordinary and special times together that promotes 'knowing' in a deeper, experiential way.

In the Old Testament, the word, "Yada," is used to describe physical intercourse; "And Adam *knew* his wife Eve." But, it means much more than just physical sex. Yada implies an experiential knowing similar to how God knows each of us inside and out with love and acceptance. What an awesome gift we give to our mates: to be truly known and considered exceptional, to have nothing to hide, and to be unconditionally bonded and accepted.

Three Keys to Deepen Intimate Companionship

If you want to deepen, build or rebuild intimate companionship with your mate, then you will need to pay close attention to three particular areas:

1. **Feelings and Attitudes:** Sharing yourself and your emotions as you build loving, forgiving, and accepting attitudes.
2. **Communicate for Connection:** Ongoing verbal and non-verbal communication with conversations that hear and accept feelings and share hearts, while also communicating through physical affection, tender looks and spiritual interfacing.

3. **Intentional Time and Attention:** Nurturing gestures plus quality and quantity time—keeping in mind that you both are special, even when the activity is ordinary.

Consider the relationship-building method *modeled by Christ* with his disciples: time and togetherness, eating, playing, working, laughing, nurturing, relaxing, travelling, talking and listening, confronting, kidding, forgiving, touching, worshiping and praying together.

Feelings & Attitudes

Unguarded Feelings

In order to know someone and be known in return, you must risk expressing your feelings and learn to be *emotionally* "naked and unashamed." This does not mean tactless dumping, but rather a secure, unguarded expression of feelings. To some people, emotional vulnerability may feel riskier than being physically naked. Emotional intimacy demands sharing your full range of feelings with your mate while also inviting and accepting

If there are Wounds...

Feeling safe and feeling "in love" is built on the foundation of a bonding Green companionship. After a trauma, or when trust has been shattered, it takes time to reestablish loving attitudes and to freely give our hearts again. Conversations and fun, easy activities will help you relearn to like each other and rebuild trust and trustworthiness. This might not be easy and it will take time and patience to develop new attitudes and skills. Consider the new growth on a gardenia bush; the new leaves that come out after a pruning are much lighter green than the more established, older leaves. Start with the lighter green growth of those pleasant feelings, connecting conversations, and accepting forgiveness.

your mate's uninhibited emotions: love, laughter, tears, anticipation, play, displeasure, excitement, curiosity, sadness, frolicking, joy, grief and even appropriate guilt and shame.

Isn't it fascinating that so many of the above feelings are best expressed by becoming child-like, embracing the freedom to be passionately accepting and innocently expressive? A child doesn't know any better than to be awed by a rainbow, curious about an unexplored playground, or delighted with an ice cream cone. A child doesn't think twice about expressing pleasure or displeasure with an immediate transparency. It is no wonder Jesus told his disciples they could not experience who God really is without tuning into the playful, uninhibited "child-part" within.

...unless you change and become like little children,
you will never enter the kingdom of heaven.
Matthew 18:3

And this is my prayer: that your love may abound more
and more in knowledge and depth of insight.
Philippians 1:9

How do you let the emotional part of you spring forth to laugh and squeal or cry without fearing judgment by yourself or your mate? What Kindergartener does not proudly display his art? But, wait a few years and the child is more hesitant to show his art, suspecting that it will not be appreciated as much as another child's art or that it will be judged as not good enough by others.

So, how do we overcome these inhibitions and unleash our feelings so that we can express them comfortably and excitedly with each other? Try doing a child-like activity together that elicits strong, spontaneous feelings. Go to an amusement park and ride a roller-coaster. Try roller skating or swinging real high at the playground. Chase each other with squirt guns. Play laser tag or a board game and allow yourself to laugh and yell in delight or scream in terror as you play.

Word of caution: This assignment was given to a couple in counseling. They came in laughing and reported a bad plan; they chose to play Scrabble and found themselves sitting in silence for ten minutes at a time, too focused on intellectual strategy and competition to embrace connecting playfulness. Choose the right plan.

I was filled with delight day after day, rejoicing [Hebrew word for "playing" and "laughing"] always in his presence, rejoicing in his whole work and delighting in mankind.

Proverbs 8:30, 31

Another way to focus on feelings is through an exercise we teach to couples as we help them listen and respond to the *feeling* part of communication. We encourage a sentence that includes: "*feel......*" and "*because.......*" Since it is your interpretation of your mate's feelings, begin with the qualifier "I hear that" or "It sounds like you feel." Your spouse can help you understand what he or she is feeling if you are off the mark. One scenario:

In the car on the way home after a weekend away...

Wife: What's wrong? You've had a real attitude today.

Husband: We only made love once the whole weekend. I've been anticipating this time away and how much fun we would have. I don't know how to make sex more important to you.

Wife: "I hear that you *feel* disappointed and frustrated *because* we didn't make love more than once this weekend and you do not think sex is important to me.

Husband: Yes, I feel disappointed. But, I feel even more discouraged and ticked off because, once again, sex wasn't seen by you as a fun way to relax and connect. I'm beyond frustration. Help me.

Wife: Wow, sounds like you're *feeling* really hopeless and quite angry *because* you don't think I view sex as fun and relaxing when I do not pursue the same frequency.

Your mate will help you identify the correct feelings, and a dialogue leading to 'knowingness' is in process! If you are at a loss, use the Feeling Words chart at the back of this booklet to hone in on how you feel and begin to expand your emotional self-awareness. Intimacy thrives on expressed feelings.

Trust and Fidelity

Feeling physically, emotionally and spiritually safe in a relationship is crucial for any depth of intimacy. Without trust, relationships stay shallow, unsatisfying and unfulfilling. Good daily choices in what you say and do can build and sustain your mate's trust. Over time, with wise choices, you can build a track record of integrity, trustworthiness and "I've got your back" safety.

Rebuilding trust after it has been broken becomes a critical process, and mates often don't realize that there is more to it than apologizing and the act of forgiving. Forgiveness and rebuilding trust are two parallel, healing journeys. Some forgiving may come first, but trustworthiness is restored and earned slowly over time. We sometimes need to ask our mate, "What can I do to make you feel safer?"

This is friendship fidelity. It may include establishing better boundaries with your parents or choosing to leave work earlier. It may mean that the more verbal spouse conscientiously leaves open air-time to encourage the less verbal spouse to speak up. Or, it may mean the more extroverted is intentional about not countering every idea with a "different thought" that could be perceived as rejecting and discounting. It may mean intentionally remembering to say aloud what you are thinking or feeling—keeping you partner in the loop. Friendship fidelity always means conveying that you value the other person and the relationship—you want to protect your intimate companion.

If you are the one who broke trust—you spoke a confidence out of turn, disregarded the agreed upon budget or in some way violated fidelity—then you are responsible for showing your remorse and repentance through deeds that can rebuild trust. This is what we call being humbly penitential. Penance is not punishment; it is the act of restoring what we have broken. Penance may include making extra phone calls to your partner, taking time to openly express appreciation and love, or writing down your passwords and account numbers. Healthily applied penance can heal both partners by demonstrating genuine remorse, which can inspire forgiveness, restored trust and the release of guilt and shame.

Thou shalt not commit adultery.

Exodus 20:14

In the present hook-up culture of the dating world, people think it normal to be physically unchaste. Instead, people regard fidelity as something that God automatically installs in a relationship upon sharing marriage vows. No! Chastity and fidelity require discipline. In friendships, we do not betray trust. We do not agree to keep a confidence or to help a friend in need and then not follow through. Daily, we must *make choices of fidelity* and practice keeping our thought-life and behaviors in line with God's intentions for a great marriage and sex life. The English word "adulterate" means to add a contaminating element, to water down or make something important less significant. We can so easily adulterate our bonding Green companionship with hurtful choices, both "innocent" and deliberate. Trust and fidelity are so critical for total intimacy.

Acceptance

Accept one another, then, just as Christ accepted you.
Romans 15:7

Whatever is true, whatever is noble, whatever is right,
whatever is pure, whatever is lovely, whatever is admirable...
if anything is excellent or praiseworthy,
think about such things.
Philippians 4:8

Many of your mate's desires, opinions and attitudes may only change with time—and some things may never be altered dramatically. In a beautiful response to these issues, Dan Allender and

Tremper Longman write, "We must see our spouses in light of what they are meant to become, without becoming bitter or complacent about who they are. Marriage requires a radical commitment to love our spouses as they are, while longing for them to become what they are not yet."[1] Too often, rather than learning to love, accept, negotiate and forgive, we allow resentment to build, we avoid necessary conflict and we start leading parallel lives instead of joined lives.

In *The Seven Principles for Making Marriage Work*, marriage expert John Gottman states that he can predict divorce if mates do not let positive feelings override their differences. They can end up with several marriage-killing negative attitudes. He calls these attitudes the Four Horsemen: Contempt, Criticism, Defensiveness and Stonewalling.[2] Contempt with growing disrespect, criticism with negativity, defensiveness with mistrust and anger, and stonewalling with avoidance can slowly creep in and poison a relationship.

Accept that your mate will have habits, behaviors and attitudes that you do not particularly enjoy. You have choices here; you can let the Four Horsemen invade or you can gracefully accept and seek out the positive. (If you can't accept, it is time to seek godly counsel.) When we marry, we marry "as is." It is God's job to change and improve your mate, not yours. A great marriage inspires many changes and much growth, but that comes after, and as a result of, a lot of healthy acceptance and taking responsibility for our own attitudes.

You can focus on each other's short-comings and build up the 'minus' column or you can choose to see the noble, good and admirable (Philippians 4:8) as you enjoy and live in your mate's 'plus' column. You married each other for many good reasons. It is a good idea to occasionally ask yourself, "What was it that made us friends in the beginning? What was it about my partner that attracted me and got us married?"

Forgiveness

Your Green Companion *will* say and do things that hurt you. Forgiving and extending grace to him or her is not optional as a Christian, especially in marriage. Forgiving is both an act of humility and an act that displays your trust in God. Forgiveness is not justice served, but a complete pardon—just as God through Christ has pardoned us. The process starts with a cognitive heart decision to forgive and is implemented with ongoing intentional choices to move beyond the grievance so healing and positive emotions can follow. It means *choosing to live in the present and not letting the past mistakes or anticipating future offenses, continually haunt you.* No one said forgiving would be easy.

Be kind and compassionate to one another,
forgiving each other, just as Christ forgave you.
Ephesians 4:32

It is important not to over-personalize the actions of your friends or mate. People often do what they do from their own immature, sinful, wounded or different internal wiring, and it can have nothing malicious to do with you. If you are hurt or crossed, consider that the person did not do it TO you, but that you may be collateral damage of his or her words or choices. As you begin to know and understand your spouse's personality, wounds and preferences, it will be easier to do this.

A final note on forgiveness: The journey into forgiving and trusting our mate must be built upon the scriptural actions of confession and repentance. Confession does not entail giving every

If there are Wounds...

Forgiving and rebuilding trust can seem impossible, especially if your mate is the offending party. Remember that these are two separate but intertwined journeys. To forgive does not mean to forget and instantly regain trust, or to justify an offense. Maintaining the relationship after certain painful wounds might be impossible, but forgiveness still brings healing. Trust can be earned as you slowly give back your heart to a mate who stops offending and shows a humble, genuine remorse, demonstrating over time that he or she is safe for you. There are occasions when you will have to make a conscious decision to keep forgiving and not pull back as you are triggered, again. Trust and safety can gently emerge and you will find yourself living more and more in the present.

sordid detail of our mistakes, but it does mean admitting our sins and taking responsibility. Confession fosters honesty and transparency. As humans we can love someone *and* also hurt them. Humbly sharing our short-comings while showing appropriate remorse can do wonders in rebuilding trust as we choose to change our offending behaviors. Repentance includes making the necessary changes to rebuild trust so you can live safely in the present.

...and More Acceptance

This is where Green Intimate Companionship meets the "Yada" experiential knowing. Reflecting your loving Father, you can study your mate to learn what he or she really wants and needs to feel lovingly accepted. It doesn't take brilliance to see that acceptance, forgiveness and understanding are foundational for a bonded intimate companionship—but it does demand courage, patience and love.

In *A Celebration of Sex*, we use two "S" words to identify some of the deeper desires of men and women: Significant and Special.[3] All of us want to feel significant and special to our mates, but Special and Significant also carry unique qualities for men and women. Husbands typically want to demonstrate strength and carry influence. They flourish on praise and respect; they especially crave feeling *significant*. Wives typically want to be someone's queen, treated as distinct, extraordinary and beautiful. Wives particularly want to feel *special*. Wives, your husband needs your admiration and respect to feel *significant* and accepted. Husbands, your wife needs your attentive appreciation, pursuit, protection and the security you can provide to feel *special* and accepted.

Nevertheless, each individual among you also is to love his own wife even as himself, and the wife must see to it that she respects her husband.

Ephesians 5:33

God has commanded husbands to love and sacrifice for their wives, while He instructed wives to respect their husbands. Why? God, our Creator, knows how we are wired. Generally, men feel accepted and appreciated when they are treated with esteem while women feel accepted and appreciated when they are cherished.

In our combined 60 years of counseling, we have seen a few common threads in what men and women say they want. We have also observed how marriages flourish when these "wants" are met by their spouses intentionally and frequently.

Men want to be respected and praised for their:
- strength and influence
- protectiveness

- passion for and successes in job or career
- completion of small tasks and projects
- generosity and ability to faithfully provide
- confidence in taking risks: decisively initiating and pursuing
- honor and integrity: dedication to keeping his word and commitments

Women want to be loved and cherished for their:

- mysterious 3-D beauty
- physical attractiveness and allure
- emotional intelligence
- nurturing and Mother Bear/Mother Hen protectiveness (Men: sometimes it may feel like she is controlling or stepping on your toes—this is unintentional.)
- team approach valuing connection and community and the sharing of those household chores
- hopes, dreams and opinions
- industriousness—cherishing how each provides
- strength and resilience in being vulnerable and responsively invitational
- uncanny intuition—a sixth sense

Rubber Meets the Road: Respect and Love Applied

A wife demonstrates her respect for her husband by being open to his desires, projects, dreams and pursuit. She may disagree or offer alternatives, but she maintains an approachable, gracious attitude. Genuine respect for her husband enables him to appreciate her need to connect, not compete. It elicits in her a warm responsiveness, sensual enjoyment, feelings of trust and safety. Remember, a wife's sexual responsiveness is heavily influenced by her respect for her husband's sacrificial, giving nature and his ability to open up to her—feeling emotionally close and special is a turn-on!

A husband demonstrates his love for his wife when he empathetically understands (which is different than agreeing) and values her desires, opinions, dreams and feelings (emotional and sexual). He considers her preferences as important as his own and does not patronize her as "too security-oriented," "too sensitive" or "too emotional." He appreciates how her unique female perspective and intuitions provide a new and different type of information. He receives her nurturing, gets some life insurance and asks for directions. Accepting and cherishing his wife elicits in the husband a deeper attraction to her total sexiness: body, mind and spirit. Attention to her 3-D allure becomes an ideal foundation for some great *mutual* lovemaking.

Note: We are not implying that if a man loves his wife enough, she will respect him enough to put out sexually and satisfy all of his sexual desires. The *mutually collaborative* sexual dance that God set in motion in marriage is much more complex and intimate than this. Women like sex, too, and want a sexual voice. A woman's respect for her husband, can bring him into a tender place of unselfishness, confidence and nurturing. And, by adoring and pursuing his wife as his special valued partner, a husband elicits a special desire in her to be vulnerable and responsively inviting. This creates a profound impact on their sex life!

Discussion Questions

1. What are some childlike or youthful qualities that you may have lost as an adult? What could you as a couple do this week that would encourage you to play together?

2. What do you need in order to forgive your mate in order to live more fully in the present? What blocks you?

3. What are some of the character traits that you might list in your mate's 'plus' column and some of the traits you would place in the 'minus' column? What action(s) will you implement to help you accept the negatives more gracefully?

4. How do you think love and respect affect lovemaking?

Communicate for Connection

God designed us to want relationships with intimate, loving connections. It is not good for us to be alone or feel alone. We build relationships by learning about each other through conversations, through affection that affirms and nurtures, and through sharing experiences which bond us together. We desire a soulful 3-D "knowing" and connection that engages all of us: our bodies, our minds with our emotions, and our hearts.

> An attentive ear can connect the heart.

Connecting Conversations

Husbands often think, "My wife sure likes to engage in a lot of unimportant chitchat." No, no. She is engaging in *connecting conversation*! A part of a great sex life is staying emotionally connected. An attentive ear can connect the heart.

In general, women ask questions to build connections while men ask questions for information.[4] Men, this means that when your wife asks you, "How was your day?" your answer needs to offer more connection (more detailed, more storied) than "Great." It is also helpful if you ask her about her day *and listen* to her descriptive answer. Try asking a detailed question about her day, and then listen in her answer for the ways that she is trying to connect with you emotionally—with her heart.

Women, if your husband tends to be less verbal you may need to help him open up by starting with questions about his work or a topic dear to him, like his favorite football team. Remember that men can quickly feel interrogated and then will get annoyed, or shut down. Sometimes conversations will come more easily if you also engage in an activity with him like taking a walk or riding to Home Depot.

Lob him 'soft balls'; make it easy for him to talk to you. Ask a question, and then be silent and count to 30. Wait patiently, quietly, as he carefully gathers his thoughts. Then listen and engage with him. You may be thinking that your husband is an extrovert who talks a lot, but even he will take some prompting to get into his deeper self.

Here's an example:

Wife: How's the land grant project at work going? The one you are working on with Pete...

Husband: [27 seconds of silence later] Pete is so slow. I'm still waiting on information from him. He may make us miss the deadline.

Wife: Oh no. Are you worried?

Husband: [17 seconds later] Yeah, Pete drives me nuts. That's why I'm home late. I had to do some of his work, too.

Wife: Sounds like a hard day. I bet you are starving!

With thoughtful questions and patient listening, you discover that your husband worked really hard today, is probably tired and perhaps a little grumpy and frustrated. You also learn that he has a really good reason for being late for dinner. He is less likely to expand further on his feelings, so he will appreciate your understanding and nurturing without feeling the need to outline every detail. With your openness and interest, he is more likely to be able to circle back around to this conversation later or to go even deeper—and make the gracious assumption that you are communicating with him to connect, rather than to control.

After the wedding vows are shared and the cake is eaten, time for romantically meaningful communication, beyond the logistics of living life, becomes a precious commodity. Most couples busy themselves with work, children, church, family, etc. You will be amazed how intimacy grows with intentional communication in those precious 10-20 minutes that you begin to set aside for connecting. You should make this a part of your daily routine and sacredly preserve this time.

- ☐ A couple decided that whenever the other came home, to stop what they were doing and go welcome them. This signaled 'You are my priority.'
- ☐ One couple with young children trained their kids to give Mommy and Daddy 20 minutes of time alone after the evening meal just to sit and talk.
- ☐ Another couple, on Friday nights moves the coffee pot to their bedroom and sets out cereal boxes and bowls on the kitchen table for the kids' breakfast. The children are told not to disturb them on Saturday morning. (Yes, they have great talks as well as …)
- ☐ Yet another couple with non-traditional schedules maps out 'Us' time each month as soon as work schedules come out, for that intentional connecting.

We cannot emphasize enough how effective Green communication not only creates closer companionship but also an enriched sex life. Learning to discuss sexual preferences, initiate and postpone gracefully, and just talking about sex together can make the difference between boring and fun. As sex therapists, we are surprised by the number of couples in long-term marriages who still haven't learned to talk about their sex life. We quickly encourage and model the ability to dialogue about this intimate topic with some astonishing results. Talk, discuss, dialogue and see for yourself!

> It is not good for man to be alone,
> I will make a helper who is just right for him.
> *Genesis 2:18 (NLT)*

Physical Affection and Tender Looks

All mammals, including humans, love to be petted and stroked because this type of touch is affirming and nurturing. Notice how we often greet friends with a handshake or hug because touch conveys acceptance and a desire for closeness. Covenant Lovers linger a bit longer in touch. There is a need to experience their bond with both the commonplace and the oh-so effective ways that lovers convey affection: holding hands, sitting close on the couch or putting an arm around the shoulder.

Maybe you are not comfortable with Public Displays of Affection. We are not suggesting excessive or inappropriate displays. Wives often tell us that an arm around the shoulder at church can mean so much; and, husbands appreciate that unexpected hug or smile of delight when they walk into the room.

It is easy to forget the behaviors that came so naturally in courtship. Just holding hands communicated so many feelings. Remember when your arm was about to go to sleep but you ignored the pain because that connection was much more important.

We also convey love through the nonverbal act of looking into each other's eyes—tender, understanding looks so aptly convey and nurture an intimate companionship. Couples can share that special look across the room while at a party that says: "You are special; I'm glad you're going home with me!"

Intentionally smile and touch more often to foster falling deeper in love (but keep it genuine). Commit to nurturing and sustaining a deep rich Green—don't let it fade!

Spiritual sharing and formation

What could be more bonding than including your mate in your most honest and deepest relationship? God is the author and catalyst of our faith and our source of hope, love and life. When couples draw from God's well of love with worship, prayer and service they will bond on a deeply spiritual and emotional level.

We learn so much about the level of intimacy shared by the Christian couples we work with by exploring if they pray together and mutually explore their faith. One couple said that it is easier to share their daily devotional before getting the kids up, and the discipline to do this has paid off. When they hit a low period, the first thing they assess is whether they have let this shared time with God slack off. Here are some activities that can help you experience God's bonding presence in your marriage.

- ☐ Attend church or small groups together and take time to discuss the sermon or lesson.
- ☐ Listen to worship music and pray together in the car.
- ☐ There are many devotional books for couples, and reading them together, even a few times a week, will help you stay spiritually connected. You can also use the scriptures in this book to move deeper into intimate connection on a spiritual, heart level.
- ☐ Intentionally pray together at optimal times like at meals, before bed, and with devotions. Include intercessory prayer for each other and the family.
- ☐ Mutually select a ministry to serve in together, or go on a mission trip. Team service builds a loving unselfishness and lets mates see the other's heart.

Remember that intimate companionship must be built 3-dimensionally with our bodies, our minds with our emotions, and our *hearts*.

Discussion Questions

1. We are better at communicating consistently and showing af-

fection when we have routines that remind us. What routines do you presently have? Or, could you create to help you deepen your intimate companionship? (e.g. Stop whatever you are doing and engage in a fifty second hug when you see each other at the end of a day of work.)

2. When could you talk to each other 15 more minutes a day?

3. Have you ever consistently prayed together? What might be the best times during the day to do so? How could you incorporate more spiritual sharing into your bonding companionship?

Time and Attention

Husbands, love your wives just as Christ
loved the church and gave himself up for her...
Ephesians 5:25

Small Nurturing Gestures

Many relational problems would disappear if we practiced simple tenderness and kindness. Be thoughtful and nice to each other. Think back to when you were dating and the small acts of love that came so naturally: "Can I get you something while I'm up?" or "Here let me rub your feet." Be intentional about doing those things continually.

All of us enjoy being attended to. Thoughtful gestures, regardless of the size, are the glue in companionship and marital closeness. They demonstrate self-sacrificing love that displays your commitment to your mate. Give small and large gifts (tangible and/or acts of service/time) to your mate suited to his or her taste and preference.

These gifts demonstrate that you seek to know, love and want to attend to your mate.

For example:

> One couple started a mutual journal right after their wedding day and kept it in their bathroom; either one could write in it at any time. Although the wife realized she wrote in it a lot more, she was pleased with how her husband appreciated reading it and did contribute. The purpose of the journal was to document fun or bonding experiences, and to share warm, encouraging thoughts with one another. When a disconnect in the relationship occurs, they find that reading the journal helps them get back on track by refocusing on the positives—not the negatives.

Quality and Quantity Time

Time spent together is the foundation of any relationship, and we make the time to do what is important to us. Couples who spend time together remain friends. Part of friendship is living, not just surviving, daily life together. Running errands and grocery shopping can be fun with a friend. Dates, mutually serving others, and chores can all become sacred times of bonding intimacy!

For where your treasure is, there your heart will be also.

Matthew 6:21

The word "sacred" means setting something apart for a specific and important purpose. Time is a precious and *sacred* gift that busy couples need to give to each other. When you give of your time it shows how deeply you care. The gift of time must be planned, set apart, reserved and guarded. Many couples think divide-and-conquer to complete household chores quickly. Yet doing the chores *together* builds bonds and can reduce feelings of loneliness.

Also, plan together time in larger chunks: one night a week, a whole Saturday every month, a weekend away every quarter and, if possible, one week a year. Busy couples cannot rely on spontaneous nurturing of the relationship. We need quantity as well as quality time.

One couple hired a sitter to come for the same night each week. It removed the pressure and burden for one of them to find a sitter. Deeply intimate couples are intentional about spending time together, staying friends and enjoying each other's company without the children or other couples along. Too many couples become business and parenting partners, more focused on responsibilities than their intimate companionship.

Mutually Bonding Activities

Seek out the experiences and activities that you found *mutually enjoyable* and bonding in the past. Many couples start to think that they no longer have anything in common. More likely, they have forgotten how to play together, have lighthearted fun, take risks and give unselfishly to each other. With a little creativity and planning, they reactivate mutual fun activities to enjoy together. Learning a new hobby or sport together can energize a relationship and help create feelings of newness (as when dating); these feelings help us to appreciate differences and awaken awareness of alikeness.

In working with married couples we often encounter this dilemma, "We are opposites and don't enjoy the same things." As we explore more creatively and think outside the box, we hear those same couples say things like:

"He prefers country music and I prefer Top 40, but we both love live music of all types and enjoy going to concerts together."

"I like to camp out, and she prefers hotels. But we both really love to hike and explore national parks, and many of them have cabins to rent. Staying in a cabin in the park works out great for both of us."

How remarkable the creative compromises couples come up with if they are willing to try something new and unselfishly release stubborn preferences. They then give their mates gifts that they desire. *All couples can discover fun, mutually bonding activities to enjoy as friends; they just need to be open to new ideas and be willing to give them a try.*

Discussion Questions

1. What would it take for you to schedule regular dates? Plan a date night right now that sounds fun to you both. Discuss who should take responsibility for arranging the different aspects of the date. Husbands, if you take the initiative, even in arranging a babysitter, you will score a lot of points.
2. Brainstorm! What activity could you as a couple risk trying that might be really fun and bonding? Laugh together about activities you try and fail, or neither one likes; you have bonded in your mutual reaction to it.
3. How might you subconsciously sabotage these dates or activities from being accomplished and enjoyed?

SENSUOUS LOVERS

Coupling Intimacy

Selecting a color to represent this very essential and often neglected category of intimacy was important to us. We did not want to choose the common pinks or blues that are often identified with masculinity and femininity. Brown and gray lacked impact. Coupling Intimacy requires a uniquely bold and sensual, a rich and royal color: Purple.

Purple intimacy is eroticism with boundaries.

Purple intimacy helps us *couple*, which means to link, attach, join or pair two items together as "an item." While Green Intimate Companionship is developed with people other than your mate, (though deep Green is reserved for your mate), Purple is exclusive to your marital companion as you delight in being sensuous lovers with that romantic, sexual attraction to each other. It adds essential elements to covenant coupling: anticipation, presence in this moment, flirtation, allure, romance and excitement!

'For this reason a man will leave his father and mother
and be united to his wife, and the two will become one flesh.'
This is a profound mystery...

Ephesians 5: 31, 32a

Purple Intimacy is eroticism with boundaries—sensuality that may be arousing, yet not having to lead anywhere. It celebrates a sexuality that is deeper and more complete than just having sex. The Greek word "eros," the root of eroticism, has a richer meaning than just sexual love with genital stimulation. Eros is *soulful* and implies a sexual force that brings lovers together in a powerful and meaningful attraction and connection beyond physical intercourse and orgasm.

Covenant Lovers can make love and feel erotically close, drawn to each other with a deeply romantic, mutual sensual bonding—without genital-to-genital contact. In the practice of Purple coupling intimacy, physical evidence of arousal may be noticed and enjoyed without further action toward orgasm. The behaviors in Purple intimacy are not for the *direct purpose* of erotic arousal, but to build sensual connection, romance and erotic allure.

Purple Intimacy enhances a romantic connection and helps you stay lovers; it adds sensual coupling experiences to Green companionship. Purple offers *non-demand* pleasuring that is playful, romantic and flirtatious. What an engaging part of sexual intimacy, to *flirt* and touch without an expectation that it must 'lead to something more'! You may be thinking, "What an oxymoron! Non-orgasmic lovemaking? How can you revel in sexual intimacy without erotic arousal and climaxes?" We encourage you to incorporate Purple intimacy in your love life; you will be surprised how exciting *flirtatiousness* can be, when arousal is the by-product and not the goal of lovemaking.

In counseling sessions, we observe that both mates tend to struggle with meaningful Purple intimacy. Men, as eternal adolescents, like sexual flirtation and feeling excited by the allure of their wives' bodies. But, the discipline of pairing up sexual enjoyment and arousal without a climax can be confusing, if not difficult. As one wife exclaimed, "Can't you appreciate the view without always touching? Or enjoy touching, without expecting more action?" Purple helps us practice being passionately present in the 'now,' instead of thinking ahead.

A female client, longing for her husband to engage in more Purple, correctly observed that he was actually cheating himself out of great quality play times by always wanting it to end in intercourse. He jokingly observed that whenever the player has possession of the ball, he is suppose to score (—not in the Purple game!). Here is an example she gave:

"When my husband arrived home from work, he hugged me from behind while I was at the stove cooking, and he fondled my breasts. I enjoyed the attention, felt frisky and was going to flirtatiously rub up against his body. But I didn't because I knew that if I did that he would want to go and make love right then, and yet the kids were there and expecting dinner. Or, he would expect to pick this up right where we left off as soon as the kids are in bed. I may be too tired by then, so I decided I should not be teasing and seductive in such moments."

How sad! Neither of them will ever know what could have happened with some fun Purple coupling!

Sensuous Purple Coupling Intimacy includes these types of behaviors:

- flirting shamelessly as Covenant Lovers
- sensuously loving with clothes on
- long, connecting hugs and kisses
- unexpectedly giving and inviting connecting caresses
- enjoying soft lighting, aromas, music and romance
- exploring, affectionate touch and massage

> Eros will have naked bodies; Friendship naked personalities.
>
> C. S. Lewis
> *The Four Loves*

You are getting the picture; it is a lot of sensuously genuine (emotional and physical) loving and flirtatious coupling—being delightfully, passionately present.

Purple, like Green and Orange, is a *continuum* from light to dark. Courting couples may engage in light lavender behaviors such as kissing, extended cuddling and caressing, but they will refrain from the deepest royal purple activities that are reserved for enriching marital intimacy.

Two Vibrant Avenues for Exploring Sensuality

Purple Coupling Intimacy is so fun. Learn to delight in and foster this crucial component of remaining connected as lovers. Zoologist and sociologist Desmond Morris made a fascinating observation that romantic couples *"pair-bond,"* and he saw that there were important sensual interactions before genital contact ever came into play.[1] He noted steps in bonding that build from Eye to Eye exchanges through to Mouth to Mouth kissing that help couples create intimate connection.

In short, for married couples, Purple Coupling Intimacy is about flirtatiously delighting in sensuality with your Covenant Lover, as you genuinely enjoy Making Love with Clothes on and Sensual Touching and Feasting.

Making Love with Clothes On

The old song "Drink to me only with thine eyes…" emphasizes a crucial lover behavior for building sensuous, intimate bonding. Fully clothed, we can make love to our mates by how we look at them as lovers.

Eye to Eye

The eyes are the window to the soul and can convey so much of what we are feeling and thinking: joy, anger, hurt, interest and amusement. We even express sexual desire through our gaze. This type of eye contact can be inviting or off-putting depending on our own mood and the condition of our marriage. Lover-companions convey healthy sexual desire and flirtation—not lust or objectifying. A direct or inviting look is often the beginning of more intimate contact.

▶ *Exercise:* Look into your lover's eyes for 1-2 minutes. Using only eye contact, convey your love and feelings.

Your eyes are the windows into your body. If you open your eyes wide in wonder and belief, your body fills up with light. ...If you pull the blinds on your window, what a dark life you will have.

Matthew 6:22, 23b (Message)

Eye to Body

We use our eyes to see and enjoy the areas and parts of our mate that we find attractive and appealing. We encourage couples to look more often and look deeper. Husbands, move beyond the obvious and revel in the femininity of your wife: her ear lobes, her mouth, her lower back and her ankles. Wives, observe and enjoy the physical features of your husband that make him uniquely attractive to you.

▶ *Exercise:* Lie naked (or with as few clothes as comfortable) in bed together for fifteen minutes as you mutually explore, experience, accept and enjoy your mate's body only with your eyes. Yes, husbands, only your eyes. Affectionate and affirming conversation can be a part of this exercise.

Hand to Hand

Our hands convey love in so many ways! They are symbolic of who we are and what we do for each other as Covenant Lovers. Imagine your lover touching you with his or her hands in intimate ways. Remember the times when you spontaneously reached out and held each other's hands and felt tingles of warm affection. Too often we forget the little displays of affection that so powerfully keep us connected as lovers over the years.

Exercise: Sensuously stroke your partner's hand. Softly explore the skin, veins and bone. Allow yourself to feel and express love and appreciation through this hand exploration.

Hand to Head

Hand to head touch conveys a special type of intimacy. No one touches our head except our mate, our mom and our kids. It is a very private and intimate part of our body. Allowing someone to touch our head means allowing an invasion of our personal space and surrendering to intimate, possessive closeness. Can you think of a time when someone lovingly stroked your face, mussed with your hair or tenderly held your face in his or her hands and spoke loving words to you?

Exercise: Relax together for five minutes each and tenderly caress and memorize the face, hair,

---

If there are Wounds...

In the present, we encourage you to re-write your story. Allow yourself to reclaim acceptance of sensual touch and feelings. You can do this by starting right where you are. Be honest with yourself and share with your mate what is safe touch for you. As you experience a safe haven of touch, allow your mate to encourage your sensuality as you begin with light Purple before progressing to more intimate touch. If anxiety arises, acknowledge it and rest without drawing away from one another. Observe where you are now and come back to the present. Resume touch, if possible, when the anxiety lessens. Purple is about mutual giving and receiving; it has boundaries with no one taking or demanding.

ears and neck of your lover.

Body to Body

Hugging body to body or cuddling in each other arms can generate feelings of emotional warmth, safety, specialness, love and unity. Close embraces release oxytocin, the bonding chemical.

People ask us what the difference is between a Purple hug and a Green hug. A Green hug is what you would give to your friend when you see each other at your community group. People would start to feel very uncomfortable if you held that hug for more than a few seconds and lingered with full body closeness. Purple hugs allow you to relax into each other and may take one to two minutes; they convey a deeper degree of intimate physical connecting.

We can include other caring Body to Body or Hand to Body intimacies like a great foot rub or a back massage. Lighter purple can be important building blocks for some great lovemaking!

Note: We include naked Body to Body hugging in the Sensual Touching and Feasting section, as those behaviors create a deeper Purple sensuousness.

(▶) *Exercise:* Hug each other for two minutes and melt into each other. Listen to the heartbeat. Relax your muscles as you feel the sensuous and romantic closeness.

Mouth to Mouth

Kissing on the mouth is a huge catalyst for sensual connecting—it is how we become and stay lovers. The Creator God put many nerve endings in our lips and mouths for us to express profound feelings. Prolonged and intimate kissing triggers erotic arousal, but the arousal can be contained as it is enjoyed. You don't have to massage your mate's tonsils, but a little tongue to tongue exploration adds to the sensuality. Relax your lips and even coach each other on how you want to be kissed. Reminisce on those early days and first kisses and times you could do this for extended periods of time. It was a major way to sensuously make love without intercourse.

(▶) *Exercise:* Kiss each other on the mouth for ten to thirty seconds. (Even 2 seconds is longer than the pecks we usually share.) Focus on being *fully* present in the sensuality of the kiss, not "what's next?" This is Purple and not Orange intimacy. Drink in the sensuous feelings and bonding emotions of deep kissing.

(▶) *Master Exercise:* Combine several of the exercises by lying or sitting with one mate holding the other in a position where you are comfortably face to face with each other. Look into each other's eyes for two minutes as you cuddle closely; now hold a tender then passionate kiss for a minute.

Kiss me and kiss me again, for your love is sweeter than wine.
Song of Solomon 1:2 (NLT)

Note: The ability to be *mindful* is critical for achieving a deeper and more passionate Purple and Orange intimacy. A simple definition of "mindfulness" would be learning to focus our minds and attention. In lovemaking, mindfulness often comes in two stages. Stage One is getting our minds and attention off daily responsibilities and into the bedroom to enjoy the process. Stage Two is tuning into our own personal sensuous pleasure. This ability to focus our attention and keep our minds spotlighted on the sensual feelings of the present moment stirs up our sensations and gives our touching exercises more intense and vibrant "colors."

For example, the experience of touching your lover's head changes when you focus your attention on your fingertips and let your body, mind and heart add meaning to those sensations. These are the lips that are soft and express love, the nose that is oily, slightly crooked and dear to me, ear lobes that are sexy, and the beautiful, silky hair that turns me on. Being mindful is allowing these many sensations and thoughts to be fully present while overcoming normal distractions. We need to anchor our attention on the pleasing touch—not judging, comparing, or losing our focus during pleasuring.

To maximize these touching exercises, intentionally practice being mindful and fully tuning your senses into the present moment. Spotlight, center, your attention on the pleasurable sensations and perhaps verbalize what you are experiencing to help stay focused. Keep your mind engrossed in the immediate experience with curiosity and acceptance while overcoming those normal distractions; your minds are seeking to achieve a stronger awareness of your body and sensual feelings. For example, you were not aware of how your legs felt sitting in your chair presently but since we called attention to it, you are now mindful of those sensations. In these touching exercises, practice being mindful and fully tuning into your senses.

Discussion Questions

1. Why do you think Purple Coupling Intimacy gets neglected in so many marriages? How do you as a sensuous lover think more Purple connecting would benefit you personally?

2. What do you think would help you as a couple more successfully make love with clothes on and ensure that Purple intimacy hap-

If there are Wounds...

and you are working on restoring safe sensual and sexual touch, lighter lavender-toned activities are a good place to begin. These might include one-minute hugs and caressing the face or hands, but not the deeper passionate Purple of deep kissing or sensuously touching nude. Incorporate more darker Green emotional sharing (maybe events of your day that allow feelings of vulnerability) while trusting your mate to handle your feelings with care. You may need to start with the physical affection of a back rub without any expectation of sensuous touching or the lighter "erotic" flirting of Purple bonding; you are re-learning that touch is safe. You may then need more time in the safety of lavender sensuous coupling, making love with your clothes on, which includes flirting and romantic attraction, but does not necessarily lead to a more vulnerable sensuality that may be overwhelming.

Going beyond Green intimacy can be scary difficult and will take deliberate choices to become sensuous lovers. Purple intimacy opens the door to enjoy romantic sensuality. Remember that feelings of sexual arousal and desire are normal but may trigger old negative feelings. Even the way your husband looks at you with natural desire can create uneasiness. Open communication about this can help separate in your mind unsafe lust from your husband's loving attraction to you. In time, you can learn to enjoy erotic feelings as you grow comfortable with your own fun flirtatiousness that feels safe and special in your relationship. Redeem your feelings of arousal and connection. Let God take away the fear and any distortion of His healthy Purple intimacy.

pens more frequently? How might you sabotage this endeavor?

3. Which of the above ways for bonding caught your attention? Which ones used to be more a part of your relationship? Which ones do you want to include more in your intimacy repertoire now?

Sensual Touching & Sensual Feasting

Have you noticed the simple, *sensual* beauty of the way our Creator God loves and provides for us? He wants to nurture our complete 3-dimensional person—attending to our physical, psychological and spiritual needs.

I don't need a thing. You have bedded me down in lush meadows; you find me quiet pools to drink from. True to your word, you let me catch my breath and send me in the right direction. You serve me a six-course dinner right in front of my enemies. You revive my drooping head; my cup brims with blessing. Your beauty and love chase after me every day of my life.

Psalm 23:1, 2, 3, 5-6 (Message)

God's love and provision for us is:

- ☐ intentional
- ☐ non-demanding and comfortable
- ☐ a peaceful, loving connection
- ☐ mindfully focused in the present moment
- ☐ bountiful and abundant
- ☐ sensually fulfilling
- ☐ unyieldingly strong and protective

What an awesome demonstration of love by our very Creator. How can we not feel love for God with this kind of attention, safety and tender generosity? As you learn to enjoy a sensual relationship with your mate, remember to model God's method of love and provision as you fall deeper in love with each other!

Sensual Touching

> Then He put his hands on her, and immediately
> she straightened up and praised God.
>
> *Luke 13:13*

In modeling Jesus, there is power to impact all 3-dimensions of a person with a *simple touch*. Our physical body, with sensitive nerve endings in our hands and arms and lips, is the dimension God uses to engage our emotions/mind and heart dimensions. What an amazing miracle of creation, to be a whole person with the ability to sensuously bond and become intimately connected through skin contact!

Research has shown that the simple act of bodily touch causes the brain to release the bonding chemical oxytocin. This chemical helps establish feelings of trust, and it lingers beyond that moment. One research study discovered that touching—through dancing— resulted in people feeling closer to each other. They also felt more connected to "something bigger than themselves."[2]

Touching and Being Touched

Comfort with touching others and being touched comes more naturally for some people. Depending on your family, culture and past experiences, touching may feel uncomfortable or awkward. But, God made all of us as touchy creatures. We humans have a "skin hunger" that needs the affirmation and comfort of healthy touch. You have experienced the difference of a warm greeting versus a warm greeting with a hug or a touch on your arm. Risking and enjoying touch helps create coupling lovers.

The good news is that you can heal from past wounds and learn to be comfortable with, and even enjoy, touch. Like most skills in life, the more you practice, the less awkward and the more comfortable you will feel, with increasing pleasure and satisfaction.

3 Levels of Erogenous Zones

Erogenous zones are areas of the body with heightened sensitivity to touch. Our erogenous zones encompass three different levels. These levels range from casual and mildly sensitive to highly sensitive and private. Great lovers are mindful of and enjoy all three levels of erogenous zones.

Level 3 Erogenous Zones:

The entire body, especially the skin.

Level 3 is our most extensive and public area of sensuality. The Creator put nerve ending in every inch of skin on our bodies. In part, these nerve endings exist to let us know when there is a cut or injury that needs attention. God's design was much more purposeful than that. Our bodies convey so many kinds of touch: caring, angry, affectionate, demanding, inviting, sensual and sexual. A mere touch on the arm or simply holding hands feels meaningful. Think about the thrill of light brushes against the skin when you first started dating.

Remember that Purple Coupling Intimacy is for attaching,

coupling and sensuous connecting, ever *mindful* of the present experience. It is not Orange intimacy with the goal of sexual arousal and achieving a climax. Purple therefore focuses on the 3rd and 2nd levels of erogenous zones.

Note: This book focuses on married Covenant Lovers. Singles will need to study scripture to determine what Purple behaviors are appropriate in their dating experiences.

Level 2 Erogenous Zones:

Sensitive areas generally not touched casually.

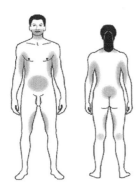

mouth, lips and face	fingertips
bottoms of feet	small of the back
backs of knees	buttocks
inner thigh	abdomen
eyelids	the navel
armpits and breast area	neck from front to back
palms of the hands	

Usually, touching Level Two areas is reserved for romantic partners in Purple and Orange intimacy. While some of these areas are not necessarily private, we do not readily touch friends or family members in those places to express loving connection. An example would be touching a person's leg. Patting the knee can be a Green connection, while a hand left on the thigh conveys the Purple sensuousness of lovers.

Level Two erogenous zones have more concentrated nerve endings and a richer blood supply, so they can be quite sensitive to the touch. God purposefully made certain areas of our body able to feel more intensely. Our fingertips can sensitively convey to our brain what we are touching and exploring—and even read Braille. Our mouth and lips have many nerve endings and it is not by chance that kissing involves these areas. Great lovers learn to maximize these wonderfully responsive parts of the body to deepen passionate companionship during sensuous touching.

Level 1 Erogenous Zones:
The MOST sensitive and private areas of our bodies.

☐ nipples
☐ genitals

These private areas of our bodies are to be reserved for our covenant mate. Highly concentrated nerve endings make them very sexually sensitive and stimulating them purposefully has the goal of erotic arousal with genital-to-genital contact and lovemaking with orgasms.

Deeper Purple coupling may include Level 1 touching of genitals or breasts but this is to be fun and any arousal will maintain boundaries and not lead to Orange. Igniting Orange intimacy, from foreplay to climaxing, focuses on purposeful arousal. God intentionally made our genitals for exciting arousal and "one-flesh" connecting—not just to create babies. How awesome to

If there are Wounds...

and you want to enjoy these deeper Purple exercises, take the time to discuss what could make them safer and therefore more sensually connecting. One mate may need to keep some clothes or underwear on at first, rather than be totally nude. Certain areas or touches that trigger discomfort or anxiety can be discussed and avoided. Again, try to stay in the present and give yourself permission to experience pleasure. Your safe covenant lover will allow you to be in charge and will stop any experience if you simply ask.

have all three levels of erogenous zones!

Active Giver/Passive Receiver Exercise

The following exercise for married couples is a great place to start to learn to enjoy touch and to fine-tune your senses. This is 3-dimensional touching that focuses on levels two and three of the erogenous zones. Purple intimacy exercises like this help us enjoy the vulnerability of intimacy and surrendering to our desire to be loved and accepted.

We want you to practice the enjoyment of touching and being touched for non-demand personal pleasure with your mate. Focus on your own sensual feelings and stay in the here and now, being mindful of your experience without judgment. Non-demand touching removes all expectations of performance. It encourages you to "just be."

☐ Allow yourself to *relax* into the touching.
☐ Do not focus on performance or arousal—*this is about perceiving pleasure with your senses.*
☐ Revel in recognizing and connecting with your Level Two and Three Erogenous Zones.

Once you begin this exercise it is best to stay quiet, allowing you both the pleasure of focusing on your own sensations and deeply experiencing sensuality. You will find that verbal communication can distract from the experience. If there is verbal communication, use it to gently coach the Giver to touch the Receiver in more enjoyable ways.

Spouses often tell us, "But I'm ticklish!" This happens at times; ticklishness may signal anxiety or that nerve endings are awakening. Sometimes a firmer touch or stopping movement for a time will help. Don't let a little ticklishness cause you to miss out. Focusing on sensations can help train the brain to experience positive, comforting and even exciting physical contact.

Purple sensuality, like this exercise, may result in physical arousal as you explore and caress your lover's body. We suggest that you define this exercise as a sensual touching exercise in lieu of erotic arousal. The purpose of this exercise can be destroyed if you allow it to become too erotically charged. The touching may then be perceived by one or both mates to be about performance, demand or arousing foreplay. Note and enjoy any 'surges' that occur, but do not act on them.

One newly married wife was concerned that her husband routinely got an erection during this exercise and was wondering what to do. To her great relief, her therapist assured her that she did not (nor did he) have to act on all of her husband's erections. His body was simply complimenting her beauty and would probably continue to do so over the coming years—and maybe at inopportune times. Appreciate those gender differences.

Wives can also discipline heightened arousal and allow the exercise to be about sensual bonding. Usually caressing the husbands body is less about arousal for wives and more about sensual nurturing and connection.

This non-demand sensual exploration is *not* foreplay with a goal of arousal and orgasm. You may make erotic love at a separate time. Instead, practice distinctly tuning into your sensual perceptions and enjoying it as a separate type of intimacy. Accept his erections and her lubrication without intentionally pursuing this reflexive arousal through to orgasm. Mindfully focus in on the sensual pleasuring and enjoyment of your bodies.

Purple pleasure is about tuning into your senses.

▶ *Exercise:* One of you will be the Active Giver or toucher, and the other will be the Passive Receiver or the one touched.

Both of you will be nude, or wearing as few clothes as you can, and remain comfortable. Set a timer for 10 to 15 minutes for touching and 10 to 15 minutes for being touched—(20-30 minutes total) so you can lose yourself in the experience without being distracted by the clock. Or, you may play a 10-15-minute play list of sensual songs.

The exercise begins with the Active Giver touching the Passive Receiver's body. The Receiver can be lying on his or her tummy while the Giver touches, strokes and caresses from head to feet; then roll over and receive touch from feet to head. Remember: the Covenant Lover will maintain a safe haven, so if there is anxiety or discomfort, signal the need to rest.

Afterwards, change roles and set the timer (or music) again. Remember, this exercise is focused on sensual touching and not foreplay with the goal of arousal, so *avoid touching breasts or genitals* (Level One zones).

The Role of the Active Giver is to:
- Caress, stroke and touch in ways that feel good to you. Attend to *your own* pleasure and sensuality of giving love while appreciating the feel of your lover's skin. Your focus is on your own pleasure, not the Passive Receiver's. However, it is helpful to know if there is a certain type of touch or place to touch that might distract from/hinder the Receiver's pleasure.
- Experiment with a variety of touches and strokes.
- Do not be offended if the Receiver falls asleep! Although sleep is not the goal, accept that your lover feels vulnerable enough to relax deeply—in time, the receiver will learn to stay in the present and enjoy.

The role of the Passive Receiver is to:

☐ Invite and accept non-demand touch until the timer goes off. Resist any temptation to give back.

☐ Focus on receiving and delighting in sensuality for yourself. Resist the negative response of feeling selfish.

☐ Increase self-awareness of your sensual body and feelings, especially those Level Two erogenous zones. Mindfully accept your sensuality, gifted to you from God

☐ Notice which areas and types of touching give more pleasure.

☐ Gain insight regarding how the Active Giver might like to be touched by noting how he or she offers touch. During the session try to coach only nonverbally and only as necessary for comfort.

After the session: Share your perceptions about the exercise. Verbally coach, in detail, about the touch that is most pleasurable to you.

Discussion Questions

1. Discuss what would help you both stay more fully in the moment during the touching exercise so that you can really tune in to your sensual feelings. Some individuals make a written list of all the things on their minds so they can set them aside with assurance that those tasks will not be forgotten.

2. What feelings did you have during this sensual touching exercise: relaxed, aroused, anxious, intimate, fearful, impatient, connected or focused?

3. How did gender differences influence the touching exercise? Men are often more aroused by the visual, while women often appreciate the sensuous closeness.

Sensual Feasts

There are many sensual ways that you can treat yourself and your partner as you enjoy Purple Coupling Intimacy. Spontaneous touch, even on private Level One zones, does not require engaging in Orange arousal and can be very flirtatious and playful.

As sex therapists, we often hear wives state: "I wish he wouldn't always grab me when we're close." We rarely hear this complaint from husbands; men seldom get upset when their wives playfully grab their fannies or their genitals. This teaches us that Purple touch can be a sensuous feast or a nuisance, depending on our attitude at the time. Husbands can help change negative attitudes, and wives can learn that being grabbed, and other "annoying" touches are, as one husband put it, "love pats with no thoughts of more, and no expectations." They are spontaneous flirtatious pursuit.

An assumption is something accepted as true without proof. Negative assumptions attributed to our mate can be quite damaging to a marriage. Wives often attribute negative assumptions to their husbands about Purple touch:

- ☐ He doesn't know how to touch without it leading to sexual arousal and release.
- ☐ I am a sexual object that he indulges in.
- ☐ If I respond playfully or allow Purple intimacy, he will want to go all the way.

A woman told us how she liked to feel alluring and be pursued, but she was frustrated when her husband would "cop a feel" when she got out of the shower and they only had 30 minutes to make it to church. She wished that his timing would be more appropriate and that he would control his Purple touching. They worked on their mutual ability to delight in his brief, playful pursuing touches and then let her go about getting ready. It became a real win-win.

If a man has recently been married, he must not be sent to war or have any other duty laid on him. For one year he is free to stay at home and bring happiness to the wife he has married.

Deuteronomy 24:5

As we move into deeper Purple and then explore Orange intimacy it can be helpful to understand how mates can bring happiness to their sensuous lover, honoring the ever-present gender differences. The art of enticing and pleasuring the opposite sex takes wisdom, effort and a desire to step out of our comfort zone. Husbands have such an opportunity to bring pleasure to their wives. But, it is not how hard they try; it is how smart they try.

What wives desire in seduction, coupling & feasting

Men, what if your wife is not that excited about sensual sexuality because you aren't attending to her preferences and making it stimulating for her? Sex therapist Laurie Watson has created some great suggestions for husbands who wish to skillfully seduce and pleasure their wives.[3] [We have added some commentary on her ideas.] This is Purple intimacy at its best. Husbands, practice some of these coaching hints and you will be amazed at the results.

☐ Look her in the eyes before you kiss her. [She desires emotional and physical connection. Don't stare at her breasts but enjoy her as a total person. Direct sustained eye contact connects with a woman's heart and sparks desire.]

☐ Tell her how desirable she is, and do it often. [Wives want to feel alluring and to be pursued. Complimenting her beauty in many natural contexts scores points, but it needs to be done when not asking for sex.]

☐ Remark on the variety of ways she is attractive: sexually, emotionally, and intellectually. [Sexy includes her personality and mind, not just her body.]

☐ Make sure she knows SHE is the object of your desire--not simply that you are horny. [The quick, direct approach can make her feel objectified. As one wife stated, "I want to be more than the life support system for the vagina." Slow down. Pay attention and make love to her. A wife can tell when you are truly present.]

☐ Tease her with your touches; make her wait for explicit touches. [Circular touches and the indirect approach is a marvelous warm-up to greater passion. Remember that cuddling and stroking create the bonding chemical oxytocin. Also, close proximity brings your wife into contact with your unique scent that releases hormones in her that trigger desire.]

☐ Use whatever resources you have to make the setting suit her preferences. [Timing, place (e.g. a warm, de-cluttered bedroom), atmosphere, being rested...so many forces work together to turn on your wife.]

☐ Be direct. Use a serious, strong voice when you tell her you want her. [Wives want masculine pursuit---not a boyish, timid approach. Develop knowledge about sexual desire, how bodies work and female preferences, because watching you "in action" as the skilled lover is erotically exciting to your wife.]

☐ Be romantic: send cards, call during the day, plan dates, and send flowers every so often. (Make a plan and put it in your Blackberry/calendar. Set a phone alert.) [Your wife loves knowing that you think of her when you are not together. It lets her know she is special.]

☐ Engage her senses: I can't overemphasize how most women like clean smells and fresh breath. Take baths together! Shave. Light candles. Simplify the bedroom to be more like a hotel room than an office or laundry room. [Great sex requires setting the stage.]

What husbands desire in seduction, coupling & feasting

Wives, what if changing two little things in your approach to lovemaking could dramatically increase your husband's sexual satisfaction and pleasure? In our workbook, *Covenant Lovers*,[4] we discuss what "Adam" wants from his "Eve" as she engages and seduces him. In fun ways, Eve can bring out her husband's sensual best. Wives, some of these suggestions may seem a nuisance or not that vital. Practice them and you will be amazed at the results.

☐ Learn to be tuned into and to be turned on by your own sensuality. [Getting beyond distractions, being fully present, and engaging your sexual voice is a turn on for him.]

☐ Flaunt your body. Revel in your passionate power and allure. [The power of female curves and genitals is "ooh, la la!" for your husband. Actively showing off your allure can be a turn on for both of you.]

☐ Assertively express your needs and desires. [Exercising your sexual voice is pursuing the sexual fulfillment God designed you to have and excites your man. Share with your mate what *you* find sensuous. It will improve his masculine pursuit of you.]

☐ Playfully grab his genitals occasionally. [We know that you wish *he* wouldn't be so grabby, but chances are he will grin at your unexpected attention.]

☐ Initiate with a provocative, teasing unpredictability. [Seductive come-ons demonstrate to him your personal enjoyment of sex. You can add variety, spice and mystery to his predictable direct approaches.]

☐ Admire his body and lovemaking skills. [Husbands love praise. Complimenting his body parts, his moves and skills at *knowing* you and turning you on motivate him even more to please you—and stokes the fire of your desire.]

In expressing Total Intimacy, the word "foreplay" might be better called "loveplay." We want lovers to appreciate all types of sexual connecting. They can enjoy Purple loveplay and Orange loveplay as they make love with *different purposes*---always relishing the journey. Appreciate the synergy of the colors!

We are often asked, "Aren't deeper Purple exercises actually foreplay? Won't Purple exercises often lead into Orange sex?" Remember, the colors are on a continuum and deep Green cuddling can blend into light Purple. Deep Purple sensuous feasts can look a lot like the foreplay of light Orange. Though Purple may sometimes lead to fun Orange foreplay and orgasms, this color emphasizes sensuous flirting and touching—not arousal. There *must* be times when Purple does not lead to or become Orange.

Try experimenting with these stimulating treats:

1. Take showers together! This can be fun and very practical. One couple would shower in the morning before going to work. Before getting out of the shower he would shout, "Shower Hug!" She would get in to start her shower and get a big, wet hug. It always stayed Purple because of the time constraints. Covenant playmates can develop strategies to boundary Purple in positive safe ways.

2. Consider hugging each other nude for a couple minutes to convey love and connectedness before putting on pajamas. Try sleeping nude. Enjoy touching genitals for exploration and learning sensuality and not just arousal. You might include talking erotically with your mate.

3. Create seductive moves as you entice your mate with your sexuality. One husband talked about how he never tired of the awe of viewing his wife's sensuous body, just like he always loved a beautiful sunset.

4. Have fun naming each other's private parts. This fun flirtation is

reserved for the exclusivity of covenant lovemaking. Having fun pet names can add shared private meaning and play to sexual interaction. Ladies, a word of advice, when naming your husband's favorite personal body part, always include the word "big" in your pet name.

5. Explore bodies and curves, making out or dancing with your clothes on to soft lighting and music. It's okay to slip a hand under the clothes at times; just remember this is about sensual coupling and not direct erotic arousal.

6. Intense kissing. We encourage you to think back to your courtship days when you made out for extended periods of time, sensuously enjoying the taste, the touch and the intimate connection. Keep the kissing ongoing!

7. Remind yourselves to be light-hearted as you play sensuously by eating food placed in strategic places. Licking chocolate syrup off tummies or nipples can be very sensual. You cheat yourself of great pleasure if it always leads to Orange—though sometimes it will happen. Share a Twizzler! Start at opposite ends and eat it, coming together mouth to mouth in the middle. Enjoy a strawberry in the same way. Linger when the lips meet.

Be creative. Plan and execute sensual surprises for your mate. Associate enticing smells, sounds, taste, and sights with your lover. Purple intimacy can embrace all five senses as you pursue sensuous coupling. Spray on a special perfume or cologne with a scent paired to you as lover. Play "your songs" as you dance close naked. Share gourmet delights and visual surprises. Flirt! Touch! Play!

Check out the "Loving with Your Senses" exercise in the Appendix; practice new, exciting level of sensuality!

Remember: deeper Purple is not foreplay and the intentional arousal of light Orange. The goal is to be passionately present not thinking of it leading beyond that "mindful" moment. Purple will be pleasurable and very sexually arousing at times, but has boundaries so your love life can remain tantalizingly sensual and sexual.

Discussion Questions

1. What might you add to the list of fun Purple activities from your own relationship? What might you like to try from the above examples?

2. Wives, what are some of your deeper desires that might be fulfilled with more Purple intimacy? Husbands?

3. How can you as a couple promote and preserve deep purple, while keeping sensual treats from progressing into intercourse and orgasms? Wives? Husbands?

Orange

EROTIC PLAYMATES

Igniting Intimacy

As we considered Igniting Intimacy, we wanted a more striking color than the usual red of Valentines, one that could more vibrantly represent husbands and wives as sexual lovers. A colleague suggested that the color orange had wonderful symbolism: **Orange** Igniting Intimacy occurs when we take the common cultural red sexuality and let the "light" of God's creative golden-yellow intimacy shine through. The result is a passionate hybrid that transforms spouses into Erotic Playmates.

Orange Igniting Intimacy can be HOT like fire! It needs the foundation of Green and builds on Purple, yet without those boundary constraints, and includes the entire orange spectrum from light peach to deep burnt orange. Light Orange foreplay can include nude or partially nude hugging and touching around the breasts or genitals allowing for increased sexual arousal (if it feels safe and comfortable). It may or may not include orgasms or intercourse. Deeper shades of igniting, erotic loveplay commonly lead to genital pleasuring and climaxes. Yet remember this is not a requirement for truly making love.

Covenant Lovers give new meaning to words like playful, alluring, passionate, tender, fun, surrender, aroused, unselfish and excited.

Exhilarating Orange Igniting Intimacy launches the synergy built by Green and Purple intimacy, and it deepens over the years. This is true 3-dimensional lovemaking as mates are "naked and unashamed" and revel in the "one flesh" connecting of their bodies, minds, and hearts with magnetic attraction and joyful excitement. Orange Igniting creatively surrenders to loveplay, arousal and passionate intercourse. This level of intimacy is reserved for and flourishes with Covenant Lovers who have pledged a lifetime together and have the foundation built by friendship, bonding, trust and commitment (Green and Purple).

Erotic Sexuality and the Bible

We sometimes wonder why the Christian church has struggled with matching up the Creator God with His gift of sexual lovemaking. Why does it seem wrong for devoted Christian husbands and wives to be erotic playmates and lovers within their covenant "oneness?" It can seem unholy somehow to play, assertively pursue, delight in and fantasize about each other and create sexual variety and fun.

What do the following scriptures tell us about erotic sexuality and Orange Igniting Intimacy? We encourage you as a couple to prayerfully think through these scriptures.

> "My lover has gone down …to the beds of spices, to browse in the gardens and to gather lilies. I am my lover's and my lover is mine…let my lover come into his garden and taste its choice fruits." "My own vineyard is mine to give…Thus I have become… like one bringing contentment."
>
> *Song of Solomon 6:2, 3, 4:16, 8:12, 10*

"Drink water from you own cistern, running water from your own well. May your fountain be blessed, and may you rejoice in the wife of your youth. ...may her breasts satisfy you always, may you ever be intoxicated with her love."

Proverbs 5: 15,18-19

"Forget about deciding what's right for each other. Here's what you need to be concerned about: that you don't get in the way of someone else, making life more difficult than it already is. I'm convinced—Jesus convinced me! ...that everything as it is in itself is holy. We, of course, by the way we treat it or talk about it, can contaminate it."

Romans 14: 13-14 (The Message)

"The husband should fulfill his wife's sexual needs, and the wife should fulfill her husband's sexual needs. The wife gives authority over her body to her husband. In the same way, the husband gives authority over his body to his wife. Do not deprive each other of sexual relations, unless you both agree to refrain from sexual intimacy for a limited time so you can give yourselves more completely to prayer. Afterward, you should come together again so that Satan won't be able to tempt you because of your lack of self-control."

I Corinthians 7:3-5 (NLT)

"Husbands, love your wives, just as Christ loved the church ... In this same way, husbands ought to love their wives as their own bodies. He who loves his wife loves himself...."

Ephesians 5:25, 28

"You are my private garden, my treasure…a secluded spring, a hidden fountain. Your thighs shelter a paradise of pomegranates with rare spices…"

Song of Songs 4:12, 13 (NLT)

"Honor marriage, and guard the sacredness of sexual intimacy between wife and husband. God draws a firm line against casual and illicit sex."

Hebrews 13:4 (Message)

"So a man will leave his father and mother and be united with his wife, the two will become one body. The man and his wife were naked, they were not ashamed."

Genesis 2:24,25 (NCV)

The Holy Trinity prioritizes intimate relationships, and God created sexuality to reveal and reflect Himself. Adam and Eve came to one another naked (without ornaments or disguises) and unashamed (moral, uninhibited and without feelings of shame or incompetence). They comfortably and joyfully revealed and knew (Yada) each other's mind, emotions and body, including their erotic sexuality and desires.

> God's verbs for our total sexuality: love and connect.

Mutual Pleasure

As we look at how God reflects Himself in our sexuality, He wants a *mutually* fulfilling relationship with us that is "unashamed"—

centered in His loving acceptance and provision. What a profound concept: *mutual.* It conveys the idea of something that is shared and reciprocal within a partnership.

Husbands and wives reflect God as they mutually focus on the other's desires and preferences to create *shared pleasure* with the same loving grace that God bestows on us each day. Sexual relating can never be self-centered. It involves mutual playfulness, a surrendering of oneself to another and to *pleasure.* It is not about taking or demanding.

The concept, pleasure, can seem foreign to devout Christians. Yet the Bible speaks often of *pleasuring* through our senses such as smelling incense, seeing beauty, touching elegant fabrics, hearing joyful noises and tasting sweet fruits. Part of God's mystery is that for pleasuring to be truly mutual, it must take into account gender differences and preferences.

Female Sexual Desire and Pleasure

We typically assume that lovemaking is preceded by a desire for sex. In other words, our sexual desire *precedes* arousal and creates the initiation. That's certainly the experience of most husbands! He thinks about sex during the day and experiences an interest in engaging in sexual activity. Then he comes home aroused and initiates —she just begins to undress and he is ready to go.

But, what about wives? A wife's arousal pattern is often very different than the pattern that describes her husband's arousal. If a wife does not feel desire prior to the initiation of sex with her husband, this doesn't mean she does not like or want sex. After talking with hundreds of women, University of British Columbia psychiatrist Rosemary Basson concluded that a wife's sexual desire often follows her arousal, rather than preceding it! [1]

Dr. Basson explains that women often begin sexual experiences feeling sexually neutral. They go on to experience desire as the result of initiation and/or the actual physical arousal triggered by the activity of lovemaking. She also states that an important part of this process is a woman's willingness to be receptive to her partner's pursuit. Barry and Emily McCarthy's definition of healthy marital sexuality includes the practice of the lower desire partner being 'willing to go along for the ride.'[2]

If a wife's desire often *follows* the initiation of lovemaking and sexual arousal, then the key to her desire is to initiate activity that she finds to be connecting if not stimulating, that can entice her receptiveness. In her book on sexual desire, Reclaiming Your Sexual Self, sex therapist Kathryn Hall, in a funny and poignant way states, "The sheer number of women disinterested in sex

If there are Wounds...

and you are beginning to desire more erotic Orange intimacy, take baby steps forward. If you were afraid to get on an elevator, what would you do to desensitize yourself from that fear? Start by observing an elevator from a distance. Then, get closer and punch the buttons but don't get in it. Then get in the elevator with a friend, but don't go to another floor. Then, go to the first floor. You can redeem lovemaking and physical pleasure in this same careful way. One wife stated she was ready for Orange Lite, a softer peach color; no orgasms or intercourse, but gentle loveplay that started with gazing into eyes and eventually led to her caressing her husband before he began to stroke her. Only then could his touch be arousing and connecting to her. Another mate stated that intercourse was permissible but only if her Covenant Lover talked to her and she could look into his eyes during lovemaking. Talk, breathe, pray, go slowly, stay in the present, be patient and play. Every journey is unique!

tells us that something is wrong. …One might wonder whether the sex available to these women is really worth being interested in."[3] Dr. Hall adds, "Implicit in the definition of desire is the fact that one must want something for oneself. Women who lack desire do not think of sex as something for them. They think of it as something they do for someone else. An important step in reclaiming desire is believing that sex is something worth wanting, that sex is something that is good for you."[4] So, what does this "truly pleasurable for wives" Orange intimacy look like?

In contrast to their more genitally focused husbands, most wives prefer a sensual caress that eventually includes the genitals but not at the outset of lovemaking. Cliff and Joyce Penner in *The Way to Love Your Wife*[5] share several insights about the type of touch that turns on the typical woman. They point out that husbands instinctively touch in straight lines while wives often want light, circular motions. Wives also like it if husbands limit same-spot touching or immediately going for the goodies. As Cliff and Joyce put it, "Don't wear it out! It is much better to leave [an exciting erogenous spot] when she wants more than to stay until she wishes you weren't there."

Finally, the caress that feels good to a wife often varies from one lovemaking experience to the next. This can frustrate husbands, who typically want to figure things out and to have a predictable plan to satisfy their wife. But, they actually will need Plan A through about S and gracefully, without pouting or shutting down, shift to Plan D or M as needed. "Oops, tonight nibbling her neck is not working (Plan H); maybe Plan C will be pleasurable to her."

A teasing sensuous stroke helps build the intensity of a wife's pleasure, but only if that touch comes with a pledge to fulfill. Husbands also need to understand that most wives do not climax during intercourse alone. They require more direct clitoral stimulation than thrusting provides. Archibald Hart, Catherine Weber, and Debra Taylor point out in *Secrets of Eve*, "… the vagina has about the same sensitivity as a man's testicles. Imagine a man trying to reach orgasm by stimulating the testicles alone…That is the equivalent for many women of trying to reach orgasm by intercourse alone. What we are stating is that you are normal if you can't reach orgasm through intercourse—most women don't."[6]

Wives tend to benefit more from leisurely lovemaking. Moving to genital touch or intercourse too quickly ensures that a wife won't have sufficient time to become aroused, experience desire and then surrender to climax. A good rule of thumb is that lovemaking should include 15 minutes of sensual touch (which does not include oral sex or stimulation directed towards orgasm) as she brings her mind and body into the present experience, and 10-20 minutes of appropriate clitoral stimulation. Wives who feel bad about taking "too long" to climax need to embrace what Shannon Ethridge in *The Sexually Confident Wife* writes: "I am worthy of the investment of time and effort it takes for me to orgasm."[7] The wife's exuberant climaxing can be a mutual, fun goal of Orange lovemaking.

In saying these things, we do not want to overemphasize the importance of female orgasm. There will be occasions when a wife will enjoy lovemaking for the emotional "climax" of closeness. She may not have the energy or wish to take the many needed minutes of focused arousal for a physical orgasm. Husbands, if your wife is not climaxing in at least half of your lovemaking experiences, then take note and encourage her to teach you how to stimulate her more effectively, as you explore together. This, too, is masculine pursuit and a way to love your wife.

We want to encourage wives to accept their desire for sexual fulfillment, know how to perceive their arousal and then to pursue it with passion. This can start with allowing yourself to fully engage in Purple sexual intimacy and mindfully experience sensual coupling. As you choose to release any internal restrictions, you can embrace and move into erotic foreplay and intentional arousal.

Sexual pleasure is an important piece of Rosemary Basson's "triggered desire" model. Since wives often do not experience a spontaneous desire for sex, memories of lovemaking experiences with their husbands that led to arousal, desire and climax in the past can trigger a willingness in the present to engage in lovemaking. Thinking about sex with these fantasies, mental imagery, can build confidence that interest and physical desire will be triggered and that lovemaking will be personally pleasurable, especially if accompanied by a loving, pursuing husband.

In summary, the path of sexual desire and arousal for a woman differs from her husband and will include more emotional arousal, a receptive choosing to engage in activities, surrendering to desire and erotic Orange intimacy. Husbands, it will often seem like you are speaking a totally different sexual language than your wife—like you are speaking German and she is speaking French. Learn some French and you will be amazed. (Wives, learning some German will be helpful, too.)

Remember the importance of mutuality and that the Creator gave both husband and wife the gift of creating sexual pleasure together in lovemaking. Sexual intimacy provides so many powerful metaphors, and God through female sexuality has much to teach us about mystery, pursuit, invitation and passion. The Creator gave women the only organ in the body designed exclusively for sexual pleasure: the clitoris. He designed women to delight in their sexual capacity and complexity as they enjoy their husband's pursuit and vulnerably share themselves out of love.

When we consider that sexuality reflects our Creator and embrace God's *perfect love,* our surrender to Him becomes less an act of will and more an impulse of love. A sacrificial and skilled husband cultivates those vulnerable, wifely impulses of loving invitation and response—and guides them into some fantastic mutual sexual pleasure.

Self and Mutual Pleasuring

God's verbs to describe our total sexuality are love and connect. He wove this into the complexity of our sensuality so that we can experience pleasure on our own (viewing sunsets, smelling flowers, rubbing sore muscles, etc.). He also designed some pleasures to be experienced when giving or receiving with another—and *most pleasure is enhanced when shared.*

Although this is true for all facets of life, mutually experienced sensuality is especially important in God's plan for our sexuality. Self-stimulation can cease to be a *relational* activity and can deter intimacy if it is not used as a means to *coach, share with, educate or assist our mate in creating mutual pleasure.* Our sexual needs and energy should drive us to our mate for mutual one-flesh intimacy; they should be not siphoned off through selfish masturbation.

Self-pleasuring is distinct from solo masturbation and can be a part of mutual lovemaking. As mates surrender to pleasure *and to one another,* they may accentuate their arousal with self-touch, experiencing a desire for a certain caress without wanting to break the moment with 'official coaching'. At certain times, husbands need more stimulation of their penis and wives need more direct stimulation of their clitoris. Additional (or timely) self-stimulation helps us to obtain and maintain arousal during loveplay.

Certain mutually enjoyed positions may necessitate mates being comfortable with stimulating their own bodies, not just their mate's body, in order to obtain heightened, igniting arousal. Self-pleasuring can assist our mate in making love as we demonstrate what touch is arousing. In fun, passionate lovemaking, couples need to get beyond who is touching what as they *mutually* engage in pleasuring themselves and each other.

The Power in Pleasuring

Wives, you have tremendous power to arouse your mate. Healthy sexual power can be actively seducing your husband by playing on his visual nature so he grins all day and you delight in your feminine power. Do a sexy dance or flash him.

The husband exerts his sexual power when he knows exactly what erotic initiation and gestures turn her on. (It probably will not be walking around naked.) It may be romantic, unexpected surprises or confidently sweeping her off her feet. As one wife expressed it, "I want him to passionately desire my femininity and take me romantically in wild and wonderful ways." As her expert lover, a husband knows how to push her buttons. This is different than demanding or taking that is not mutually playful or arousing.

Experiencing our mate getting turned on by our sexual allure and power is a big turn on for both lovers. Power used rightly is never manipulative but always win-win. Don't stifle your excitement and playfulness from fear and inhibitions. It is a gift to your mate to use your sexual power and create that Igniting Orange synergy!

Props and Variety

We often get questions about whether it is permissible for Christian couples to use sexual toys. Our preference is to expand the definition of toys, which are often battery operated, to a broader idea of *props*. Props can be anything that may assist in enhancing the experience of mutual lovemaking.

Props can stimulate ambiance or bring variety. A prop of flickering candlelight with soothing music in the background will create a totally different mood than props of mirrors employed in an afternoon delight with stirring jazz playing on the stereo. Clothing, which is also a prop, provides endless opportunity for sexual expression: sexy lingerie, red silky boxers with hearts, a dress shirt and nothing else, a favorite nighty or a form fitting T-shirt and cut-off shorts.

There are common household items that can be used as props to increase pleasure. Pillows are great to lean against or to help support certain sexual positions. Everything from feathers to fruit and perfume to satin gloves, offer an increased awareness of the five senses. Scented lotions and oils can be kept handy along with your favorite lubrication. Note: You may need to find the right quality of lubricant that reduces friction, does not dry out quickly, and isn't a spermicidal. For inexperienced newlyweds or post-menopausal women, a lubricant with silicon (like Wet Platinum, etc.) or natural oils (Radiant Love Butter) may be more effective. Be aware of allergies and read labels.

Some couples worry that certain props will create sinful desires, imitate porn or detract from what God has designed as natural attraction and arousal. A husband wasn't sure if his wife's sexy dance and seductive lingerie were okay or if it was a distortion of God's design for sexual allure. One Christian wife said that when they rearranged their bedroom furniture, the dresser mirror was positioned so they could see themselves making love. She was alarmed that this might be wrong because she enjoyed the sexual excitement it stimulated for her. Here are some guidelines for using props. They should:

1. be kept playfully in perspective and be adjunct to, not the

focus of lovemaking—never becoming the center (a fetish) of sexual arousal.

2. promote a 3-dimensional expression of your sexuality that involves body, mind and heart-felt emotion. It should never encourage your loveplay to become physically one dimensional—simply a buzz.

3. never invite ideas of someone else into your bedroom as pornography does. It should always be focused on your relationship.

4. be used in ways that are *mutually* fun, invite vulnerability and enhance passionate intimacy in your God-given role as erotic playmates. It should increase the ability to exuberantly surrender the responsibilities of the day and focus on one another without anxiety or discomfort.

Mental Imagery and Fantasy

Great lovers liberally employ their greatest sex organ: the brain. God expects us to use our minds and imagination. He created humans with a need for stimulation, adventure and variety. Sexual imagination can provide all three. Although God intends for you to use your mind, He also expects self-discipline. Any thought or behavior that detracts from enjoying, protecting and valuing *your* mate is wrong and falls outside God's blueprint for building intimate companionship and a great sex life.

Be careful what you think, because your
thoughts run your life.
Proverbs 4:23 (NCV)

Fantasy, also called mental imagery, means applying our God-given creative minds and imagination to our lives. We fantasize and create pictures and stories in our heads about what we desire: the house we want to live in, how many children we will have, and how our sex lives will play out. Our fantasies tell us a lot about who we are, what we need and what we want in life as well as how we may need to grow and change to be more fulfilled.

Understand that your sexual fantasies and imaginings are to be focused exclusively on your spouse and kept within God's sexual guidelines. Your spouse should be the star of your mental movies. These mental images are not lustful or sinful because they are *not* coveting what you do not have or entertaining thoughts about things that you wish your spouse would do but never will. Sexual fantasy is simply allowing your creative mind to enrich *your shared sexuality*. You are building private and mutual mental images—not borrowing images from someone else, like porn does!

Do you know the saying, 'Drink water from own rain barrel, draw water from your own spring-fed well'? It's true. Otherwise, you may come home one day and find your barrel empty and your well polluted. Your spring water is for you and you only...

Proverbs 5:15-17a (Message)

It is important to note that your mate's fantasies about things you have not done (or will not do) does *not* imply that you are not enough or that you are doing something wrong. Instead, sharing your imaginative thoughts with each other can help make your marital lovemaking richer. It keeps you vulnerably connected, keeps sex on your radar and introduces you to fresh ideas as well as reminds you of the previous experiences you enjoyed together. Learning about each other's sexual imagery, without demand or obsession, will deepen how well you know one another, and help you decide what you mutually wish to include in your lovemaking repertoire.

Dialogue and discuss:
- ☐ Are your mental "movies" similar?
- ☐ Are you willing to experiment with your mate's ideas? Why or why not?
- ☐ What do you learn about your mate when listening to his or her fantasies?

Men's fantasies, in general, focus on Level One erogenous zones and explicit sexual activity. He is turned on by the visual stimulation of his nude Eve and touching her genital area. Eternally childlike, he is curious and enjoys unexpected adventures and variety in his fantasy life.

Women's fantasies, on the other hand, often encompass a full body and mind experience: enjoyment of emotions, ambience, romance, the personality behind the body and the sexual activity. She revels in the relational pursuit and overall sensuality. She appreciates male attributes but does not tend to focus on his body parts in her fantasy life.

We recommend reading books on sex together to stimulate fun conversations and discover some new things to try. Here are some books written by Christians.

A Celebration of Sex, Douglas Rosenau
Sheet Music, Kevin Leman

When Two Become One, Christopher and Rachel McCluskey
The Way to Love your Wife, Clifford and Joyce Penner
The Sexually Confident Wife, Shannon Etheridge
Intimacy Ignited, Dillow and Pintus

You'll find a longer list of resources at www.covenantlovers.com.

Sharing *all* of your fantasies with your spouse is not necessarily wise, especially if you know that it is something that would make your spouse uncomfortable or is truly outside God's sexual economy. However not sharing *any* of your sexual imagination with your spouse and not building fun fantasies together will likely diminish your love life. Moreover, discussing your fantasies may be arousing. It can also be fun to play out some of them. Spread out a blanket and make a sensual picnic; rub suntan lotion on one another and pretend that you are at the lake or beach without ever leaving your bedroom!

A great fantasy life and a dynamic sex life are, indeed, a state of mind. Let the Holy Spirit ignite and convict your mind. Unleash your childlike wonderment and curiosity as you discover new dimensions of play through mental imagery. Try sharing your *ideal lovemaking scenario* with your spouse, and playfully think through how you might bring some of those ideas into your lovemaking. Using your imagination can lead to light-hearted laughter and a bonding closeness.

Non-demand Genital Exploration and Pleasuring

An important part of Orange Igniting Intimacy can be genital pleasuring for the purpose of understanding and enjoying your mate's body, connection and *arousal* without necessarily leading to intercourse or orgasm. This pleasuring goes beyond Purple intimacy. It is a focus on the genitals, though the goal may be less arousal and more creating knowledge, closeness and anticipation.

Let these concepts stretch your thinking:

- [ ] non-demand genital pleasuring that enjoys heart-sharing, vulnerable connection with possible arousal while postponing orgasms
- [ ] intercourse that lingers in the physical oneness without the goal of a climax

Couples find that interspersing intercourse without climaxing throughout their lovemaking can be a turn on. A woman once told us that the first time she ever felt that she and her husband truly made love was when he slowed down and allowed many minutes of holding her in an intercourse bear-hug without climaxing.

Certain positions of holding each other foster non-demand genital pleasuring. For example, sit with your back against the head of the bed with pillows propped appropriately as your mate settles between your arms and legs and leans back against you. This allows you to caress her or his nipples and genitals. You could also sit facing each other with legs over each other, placing genitals in a comfortable reach for pleasuring.

As Christian sex therapists, we encourage married couples to keep discovering new things about each other and prescribe the following exercise for newlyweds and longer marrieds. The goal is to have a greater knowledge of what creates sexual arousal and passion in your mate---to be able to encourage genital interaction throughout the lovemaking process that increases pleasure.

▶ *Exercise:* Let the husband get into a comfortable position lying on his back. The wife will gently and carefully explore and touch his genital area from perineum (skin between anus and scrotum) to the tip of his penis. Caress scrotum and testicles; explore the penis both flaccid and erect. Let him tell her what feels especially sensitive and arousing. Switch places: let the wife lie on her back and the husband does the same, taking time to explore what feels best in the vagina as well as both the inner and outer labia and clitoris. Pull the clitoral hood (top of inner labia) back and notice the clitoris—massage it to greater arousal and feel the clitoris become erect. Tell him what feels especially sensitive and arousing.

How fun it is to be a student of your mate's body. Keep the experience safe; do not pressure a mate to explore or be explored beyond what is comfortable to him or her. Keep interactive conversations alive. Remember, this is *mutual* pleasuring. This attitude enables couples to 'stretch' and try different things. Orange Igniting Intimacy and mutual pleasuring has such variety with so many dimensions. Celebrate!

Discussion Questions

1. Are sexual assertiveness and creativity OK with God? How do you as mates feel about creating variety and engaging in new behaviors? When and how might you cross the line into counter-productive attitudes or activities?

2. What could Covenant Lovers do to help the wife assert her sexual voice? How do you as a couple "trigger" your wife's desire? Wives, what could your husband do? What do you need to do for yourself?

3. What sexual props do you use to enhance intimacy? Add to our list some props that you might want to try.

4. What sexual memory do you have of a special time in the past that you enjoyed with your spouse? Share!

5. How do you think Orange Lite (non-demand genital exploration and pleasuring), could increase the passion of your sex life?

If there are Wounds...

some of the suggestions for Orange intimacy will need to be processed with your Covenant Lover as the two of you redeem erotic playfulness and passion. It is difficult to know when to push through some discomfort, or when you will risk more hurt. Everything from language, to nudity, to certain props, to thinking of mental pictures, to genital arousal can trigger past pain. Become more aware of what you are experiencing in your thoughts, emotions and body responses and then share it with your partner. This journey will take time, love and discernment. At any time you may ask to go back to safe Green and Purple activities to maintain intimate connection. Orange intimacy can at times seem more like working on sexual healing than an active pursuit of desire and arousal.

Problem-solve: How can this touch or activity be made safe? Are you ready for more arousal? Be patient yet bold. God wants to give you your own unique and pleasurable sex life. You are special agents of healing for each other. One husband commissioned himself as his wife's Special Agent to help her find her sexual voice and sexual healing. Pray for the wisdom and courage to do that which initially feels uncomfortable. Both must guard how far to stretch. Talking and being vulnerably transparent can build trust and a safe surrendering. Trying things, moving forward and then backing up, processing, growing and healing is a journey for most couples.

Sexual wounding does not have to be a death sentence on Total Intimacy evolving into meaningful lovemaking. Couples who have to work through pain and trauma to achieve sexual intimacy develop powerful skills that will enrich their covenant connection over a lifetime. Even the deepest Orange can be a vital component of your sexual journey toward healing and mutual pleasure!

Continuum of Lovemaking

You may never have thought about putting your involvement in lovemaking on a continuum, but we have all experienced these various levels of involvement. It may have confused you or even felt uncomfortable to acknowledge. On one end of the scale, we have had experiences where one mate was not that interested; it seemed very much like pity or duty sex. Maybe other times it started out as a choice to nurture the other and the sexual arousal turned into desire and the lovemaking moved into being mutually connecting—even passionate.

Remember that the definition of Total Intimacy includes complete and fulfilling lovemaking. This is why we have chosen words like nurturing, connecting and passionate to describe this continuum. The lower end of sexual involvement, sex out of duty or pity, needs to be avoided as a losing proposition for both lovers.

We created this chart to construct a language and concepts to help you improve your understanding of lovemaking. The goal is to help couples avoid building up resentment and misunderstandings. Use this tool to assess, accept and appreciate your present sex life, and use it to improve your attitudes and behaviors involving God's design for it.

You may want to keep this chart near your bed so you can point to the kind of lovemaking that you anticipate or have the energy for this time. The continuum ranges from: "Yes, honey, I'm totally fried, but I would enjoy nurturing you" to "I'd love you inside me but don't need an orgasm tonight" to "I can't believe God made you so gorgeous, we've got 30 minutes—let's get naked!"

Continuum of Involvement in Lovemaking

PASSIONATE	CONNECTING	NURTURING	DUTY	PITY

10　9　8　7　6　5　4　3　2　1　0

{ MOST LOVEMAKING }

0 – 1	PITY	motivated by guilt, frustration, begging or to avoid conflict, neither partner enjoying any real intimacy, leads to resentment by one or both
2	DUTY	marital obligation; meeting physical needs without real satisfaction, does not foster true intimacy
3 – 4	NURTURING	honoring need of higher desire mate, done willingly with various levels of participation and fulfillment
5 – 7	CONNECTING	warm, slow, playful and tender; may slide across the continuum from nurturing to passionate
8 – 10	PASSIONATE	more intensity, focus, time, orgasms; thermonuclear "wow" sex!

Good Sex or "Wow" Sex?

Though couples may fantasize about incredible, thermonuclear sex that happens spontaneously and with great frequency, the majority of enjoyable lovemaking in a healthy marriage is in the 3–7 range with nurturing and connection as the important goals—and most often actually do include orgasms for one or both mates. It is not uncommon for wives (or husbands), to start on the lower end of 3 yet end up at 6 or 8. One wife with two young children stated honestly, "I like sex but am good for wow sex (8-9) with lingerie and orgasms about once a week."

Sex isn't a passion or frequency contest. Relax and enjoy. Your erotic lovemaking should permeate your relationship and manifest itself in all kinds of ways. Remember the 3-dimensional goal: *bodies* express affection and excitement; *minds* create amazing feelings and choices to engage as your *heart-felt* union energizes staying in love and reinforces your desire to wrap your arms and legs around each other. In combination, with consistency and kindness, they reflect God's *heart*.

When sex therapists Barry McCarthy and Michael Mets write about "Good Enough Sex," or GES, they do not mean settling for a boring, mediocre sex life:

> "The GES we're talking about is *realistically great sex* that serves a number of purposes in our life—pleasure, tension release, self-esteem, emotional intimacy, and /or reproduction."[8]

> They summarize the overarching principles of quality couple sexuality and good-enough sex as, "to develop a mutually comfortable level of intimacy, value pleasuring, integrate erotic scenarios and techniques, and establish positive, realistic expectations as an intimate team."[9]

Couples stuck in pity and duty sex need to work their way up the scale. Pity and duty sex can happen, for example, especially if the couple is unintentional in their relationship. They may have neglected Green and/or Purple. Or lovemaking may have become just another activity to check off the task list. In time it feels like a chore or one mate feels sorry for the partner who needs 'release.' It is a lose-lose situation for both spouses and can kill intimacy and the relationship.

If one or both of you are not able to gracefully say "No" when you are not in the mood, then you will not be able to authentically say "Yes" when you are. Remember, a lover saying "Not tonight" is not a refusal; he or she is simply *declining* or *postponing* lovemaking until a better time. The difference between good and bad sex is often honest communication and realistic expectations; "I'm genuinely interested in 4 and enjoying our connection but please do not be offended if I do not match your 8."

Nurturing (3-4) lovemaking can be mutually fulfilling but again, it will depend on your attitudes. Many husbands, perhaps trying to be unselfish, insist that they cannot make love unless their wives can fully engage and have climaxes, too. Many wives in our counseling offices have pled that they don't want an orgasm every time. Sometimes they may be too tired or simply do not need to go for fireworks. They do deeply desire the sexual connection of love-play and of having their husbands inside of them. Wives do not want their husbands to incorrectly think that they are not enjoying the sexual experience but they get turned off if pressured to go after an activity they do not want or feel they can achieve at that time.

Simple rule of thumb: a wife enjoys a climax at least 50% of the times you have sex.

Often wives are willing to manually or orally pleasure their husbands to release as they enjoy mutual nurturing.

Giving up unrealistic expectations and knowing that much of your erotic playing will take place in the very fulfilling quality area of 3-7 can give your Orange Igniting Intimacy new meaning. We think you will develop a richer and more meaningful depth of lovemaking as you give each other permission to enjoy the full spectrum of sexual expression and ways to feel close and nurturing throughout the continuum.

Don't give up on "wow" sex, though! We need that, too. Passionate, wow sex (8-10) often takes a convergence of many factors: time, anticipation, variety and privacy, strategic props and environment, uninhibited positive feelings and mutually building arousal and climaxes. Just remember that lovemaking can have many different and fulfilling objectives that create great marital satisfaction.

Discussion Questions

1. What can Covenant Lovers do to keep the duty and pity sex to a minimum? Discuss how you could gracefully decline or postpone without frustrating your mate.

2. Why do you think having realistic expectations for your sex life is important? Do you agree that most meaningful and even great sex takes place between 3 and 7 on the continuum? Is 3-4 okay?

3. When was the last time you had "wow" sex? What were the factors that helped that occur?

Types of Lovemaking

We have intrigued you, we hope, with the immense variety of sexual excitement and connection in Orange intimacy. Sometimes Orange will feel like a bonfire out of control and other times a cozy camp fire, a brilliant sunrise or a calming beautiful sunset. As erotic playmates, you can experience many different degrees and shades of lovemaking. We have grouped some of these into three categories with eight types—knowing they will often blend together and not always be distinct.

Igniting and Bonding Lovemaking

IGNITING AND BONDING	IGNITING	BONDING
1. Teasing Prelude	4. Quick Encounter	6. Playful Romp
2. Fantasy Enrichment	5. Erotic Volcano	7. Nurturing Release
3. Gourmet Marathon		8. Connecting Companionship

This first category of loveplay ignites strong feelings with fun arousal. It also bonds couples together as lovers. Romance and feeling in love requires a special, exclusive connection that flirting, fantasy and gourmet marathons keep vibrantly alive.

1. Teasing Prelude

Ideally, this permeates the atmosphere and relationship of a great marriage 24/7! Be seductive. Flirt and give compliments. Drink in visually and touch strategic parts briefly. Include a lot of Purple intimacy with a definite Orange flavor as you tease and anticipate. This type of lovemaking keeps mates lovers with sexual energy, attraction and pursuit on the front burner, rather than 'drifting' into roommates.

2. Fantasy Enrichment

We have emphasized that the mind is the most crucial sexual organ for great lovemaking. Use it. Reminisce. Dream up a lovemaking scenario to enjoy. Remember something your mate told you was a real turn-on. Go back and recreate some favorite times from your mental movies. Try something new!

3. Gourmet Marathon

The fun goes on for at least an hour. All 5 senses are emphasized. The tempo varies from intense to languid. Intercourse and orgasms are included along with conversations, eye contact, a lot of holding and caressing and maybe some strategically placed food. Wow sex at its best! Go for that 8 to 10 on the continuum.

Igniting Lovemaking

God designed 3-dimensional human beings to fall in love and enjoy wildly exciting sexual experiences as Covenant Lovers. He created orgasms to bring an amazing level of sensory fulfillment.

4. Quick Encounter

Enjoy an adventure and have some spontaneous fun. This is a quick, time-limited, often spontaneous, jolt that adds spark to an already enjoyable sex life. One or both partners may experience a climax in these few minutes of connecting and can walk away with a grin on their faces and in their hearts.

5. Erotic volcano

Climaxing gives us a profound experience of what can happen when the body, mind and emotions synchronize. The erotic volcano is focused sensuality and intense feelings: teasing prelude, erotic build up, focus on personal pleasure, emphasize groans, tense muscles, heavier breathing with abandoned inhibitions, surrendering to the explosions!

You may want to have a "husband fun night" or "wife fun night" and focus totally on his or her pleasure. God created mates to share sexual apexes!

Bonding Lovemaking

This category, more than any of the other categories, epitomizes erotic playmates. Remember, good and great sex occurs most often on the continuum from Nurturing 3 to a Connecting 6 or 7. Value and appreciate nurturing, playful, connecting lovemaking. What a gift from our creative God to help us recreate, release tension and feel intimately close.

6. Playful Romp

The definition of romping is "to play in a boisterous way." This is the epitome of childlike playfulness with lighthearted laughter and simple, spirited fun. Great sex often takes place in our child-ego state—the child part of us that stays curious, is awed by the unexpected, accepts easily, expresses feelings spontaneously and loudly, and needs to play. Remember to squeal and groan and express yourself uninhibitedly. Covenant Lovers romp and play together in frisky, boisterous ways for a lifetime of entertainment.

7. Nurturing Release

You are open to sex and open to feeling close. You want to honor your partner's wish for connection and release. One spouse may not feel like an orgasm, so do not insist. The result is often more than a hormonal release of sexual tension; our *God-given need for intimacy is being fulfilled.*

8. Connecting Companionship

Sometimes sex just needs to secure a warm, comfortable closeness. This is "one flesh" lovers feeling intimate and tenderly "naked." Connecting lovemaking (5-7 on the scale) comes alive with being comfortable, loving sexual playmates. This connecting sexual companionship can be motivated by a mutual desire to come close, with each mate having their different needs met. This creates a beautiful example of non-demand, pleasuring tenderness.

Brakes and Accelerators to Lovemaking

What a wonderfully beautiful gift God has given us to become erotic playmates. How then can you make your erotic Orange even more passionate as you engage in all eight types of lovemaking? What are some of the busters and boosters, the bombs and builders, of a great sex life? Here are some of our observations over many years as marriage counselors and sex therapists.

Common Brakes for Wives:

☐ **Fatigue:** husbands often underestimate the effect of tiredness on a woman's libido, though that can be the number one issue we encounter in helping women enjoy lovemaking. This includes the tiring effect of children, work demands, and family responsibilities.

- **Body image:** all women experience the interfering toxin of negative comparison at times. What a brake to a great sex life as wives usually find some part of their body unattractive.

- **Distractions:** a messy bedroom, family problems, phone alerts and kids knocking on the door can interfere before and during sex; women's brains multitask better than men's brains but also are more susceptible to distractions that can pull them out of the moment.

- **Relational shortfalls:** neglect and lack of accessibility, emotional distance with little companionship or pursuit can shut down a woman's ability to respond; a wife wants to feel alluring and emotionally connected to her husband in order to vulnerably surrender herself and her body.

- **Mutual skill deficits:** a wife neglecting her sexual voice and a husband overlooking his need to wisely pursue and arouse his wife—boring or uninteresting sex results in avoidance and inertia for both.

Common Accelerators for Wives:

- **Make it all about her:** rather than pursuing a hormonal 'need' for release, husbands can pursue and make love to their wives on all 3 dimensions (stimulating her body, creating emotional attraction and arousal, empathetically connecting hearts), while wives seek and enjoy their own sexual pleasure and arousal.

- **Affirm the body:** husbands should continually compliment, pursue and appreciate their wife's 3-D beauty; wives must be willing to accept and believe these compliments—you can fashion a positive body image and buy into God's verdict that you are wonderfully created with just the right body to create and experience a great sex life with your husband.

- **Get rest and minimize distractions:** sharing chores and child responsibility, encouraging her to nurture herself with a hot bath or a manicure, picking up the bedroom, turning off the technology, taking the initiative to arrange for a sitter—all these can be tremendous aphrodisiacs for an overwhelmed wife.
- **Include much flirting and romance:** Purple works with daily looks and touches, a husband's attention to his wife's world, phone calls, those unexpected surprises, candles and flowers, lingerie of her choice, and the list of romantic gestures can go on and on.
- **Practice skilled initiation and lovemaking:** a wife is turned on by a confident husband who will sweep her off her feet through his understanding of how to trigger her desire and pleasure. He initiates and promotes her involvement in passionate lovemaking.

Common Brakes for Husbands:

- **Lack of visual, psychological and physical stimulation:** a husband's arousal can get short-changed because he is more easily turned on. Wives can neglect the mutual pleasure of engaging their husbands with sensuous touch, lingerie, compliments, nonverbal exclamations, and attention to their Level One erogenous zones. Sometimes focusing on him can slow down the lovemaking process in helpful ways.
- **Rejection and inertia:** husbands get discouraged and insecure by repeated postponements. They can perceive it as a rejection and the fallout can be abandoning their role of initiation; then a sex life at rest tends to stay at rest and dig a deeper rut—but like the law of inertia, a lively sex life stays in motion and builds speed.

- **Emotional blocks:** anger, stress, anxiety, grief and fear can all interfere with a man's libido; his testosterone will not break through every barrier. Addressing his negative feelings can be critical for getting back to meaningful lovemaking.
- **Relational turn-offs:** a negative or disinterested wife can feel like sleeping with the enemy. Duty or pity sex is always a turn-off; a common brake is a wife who has not developed her own sexual voice and is resigned to servicing her husband.
- **Distortions:** pornography with its self-medication and escape, affairs, siphoning off sexual energy with masturbation, no pursuit of healthy Total Intimacy with a fear of the necessary commitment of time and energy, insecurities and skill deficits can all become a kiss of death to intimate lovemaking.

Common Accelerators for Husbands:
- **Becoming an enthusiastic naked lover:** what a turn-on!—a wife who embraces and celebrates her feminine power with zest in all types of lovemaking; a wife who is very interested in sex because they have mutually made lovemaking very attractive and fun.
- **Practice ego boosting, affirmations, initiation:** husbands never tire of praise and hearing that "I'm so glad God chose you to be my Adam—what a lover!" Or "Goodness, you're so big." He appreciates a wife who enjoys lovemaking enough for herself that she pursues, initiates and focuses on his body too.
- **Enjoy laughter and passionate non-verbals:** grinning, groaning, winks, laughing, seductive looks and playing are such aphrodisiacs. Green and Purple are so foundational to great sex and being erotic playmates!!
- **Employ adventure and variety:** it is a turn on for a wife to plan

sexual surprises and encourage new and varied activity in different settings (e.g. the car in the garage instead of the bedroom, the kids at grandma's and eating supper nude)—that is why God gave us imaginations. How interesting that this excites not only the husband but the wife as well.

☐ **Stay healthy and exercise:** discipline with diet, sleep and exercise improves lovemaking—a healthy body can prevent erectile difficulties and provide the energy for some fantastic lovemaking.

☐ **Create frequency:** planning and taking advantage of optimal times—so often there are those 3-5 times a week possible for lovemaking and if you do not schedule a couple, you will slowly become roommates and parenting partners, but not remain lovers. Frequency does not have to be a performance goal of a certain number of times a week but rather a resolve to keep lovemaking on the front burner and prevent inertia from set-ting in. Planning in a meaningful sex life does not have to eliminate spontaneity, as you nurture creativity and variety during those sacred (set apart) times.

Be honest! So many of these brakes can be avoided with intentional, wise choices and putting some effort into your marriage. And, you already know and practice many of these accelerators, but maybe just not consistently enough.

Like Jesus often encouraged, "*Go and do* the things I have told you." Great sex lives do not just happen. You will need to employ in your lovemaking some courage, discipline and the love we know you have for each other. Make deliberate choices to spend time together. Learn and practice new skills until they become comfortable as you speak both French (wife) and German (husband). Include a lot of Green and Purple in with your Orange intimacy—creating Total Intimacy is so rewarding.

We encourage you to remain ever *intentional* in your relationship. One couple writes 'SNAP' on their calendars one or more times each week. It means 'sex and a nap'. They set aside this time to enjoy each other and practice the accelerators. It is left open-ended as to whether it will be a Green, Purple, Orange event with the fabulous synergy they each can create.

Summary Suggestions for Igniting Lovemaking

Here are a few reminders to help you and your covenant playmate trigger passionate, thermonuclear or warm, connecting lovemaking. Think through how these can be applied to your love life.

☐ Promote mutuality and show respect with erotic behaviors.

☐ Learn to say "No" so you can joyfully say "Yes." Learn to say "Yes" so you can unselfishly say "No."

☐ Loveplay vs. Foreplay: Be playmates 24/7, not just when you want sex. Don't underestimate the importance of extending the loveplay.

☐ Focus on and stay in the present. Be personally *mindful* in your sensuality.

☐ Intersperse intercourse and orgasm within your Orange pleasuring. While intercourse and orgasm are an important aspect of sex, they are not the whole deal. Building and basking in oneness is the ultimate goal of all passionate lovemaking.

☐ Develop your comfort with and skillfulness in mutual genital pleasuring.

☐ Prepare an ideal atmosphere: safe, sensual, comfortable and romantic.

☐ Revel in the distinctiveness of your gender and your spouse's gender. Enjoy the distinctiveness of your Covenant Lover as you empower his or her *personal sexual voice.*

☐ Talk before, during and after lovemaking---enthusiastically express your excitement and pleasure verbally and nonverbally.

☐ Read books (okay maybe a chapter) on sex together and apply the knowledge through honest discussions.

☐ Include a lot of Green and Purple Intimacy as you live life together and stay in love.

Slow down, surrender control and enjoy God's gift of sexuality. Our sex life is not a performance exercise! If we rush through it we will miss the beauty of the intricate creation of our different bodies and their ability to respond with delightful sensuality.

The marriage bed must be a place of mutuality—the husband seeking to satisfy his wife, the wife seeking to satisfy her husband.

1 Corinthians 7:3

Honor marriage, and guard the sacredness of sexual intimacy between wife and husband.

Hebrews 13:4 (The Message)

Discussion Questions

1. How are the different types of lovemaking important in a vibrant sex life? What might *each* uniquely contribute to creating the passionate love life to which a great marriage aspires?

2. In order to fully enjoy a Gourmet Marathon, in what ways can you tune into your sensuality and enjoy the present rather than rushing on? Wives, how might you help your husband

enjoy his erection without orgasm while you both become more fully aroused?

3. Explain and expand on two of your personal brakes and accelerators that you wish your Covenant Lover could attend to better. What has sabotaged your efforts to change these in the past?

4. How would you prioritize the tools, suggestions, for igniting a great sex life? Which ones do you think you as a couple need to practice more to become the passionate erotic playmates God designed you to be?

A Prayer

Write a benediction for your sex life as Covenant Lovers. A benediction is a closing prayer that asks God for help, guidance and blessing. The Almighty chooses to be moved by our prayers and petitions. He chooses to create and add abundance to each marriage as we pray specifically.

☐ Recount some areas of growth in your sex life for which you are thankful.

☐ Identify areas you would like to grow or to heal in your lovemaking.

☐ Pray specifically, as covenant playmates, for the wisdom to empower each other's unique sexual voices, as you mutually celebrate God's gift of lovemaking.

☐ Thank God for your spouse and the gift of masculinity/femininity and a rich love life of Green, Purple and Orange Intimacy.

Our prayer for you is that Total Intimacy will flourish in your lovemaking as you reflect God's love and celebrate the sexual privileges and pleasures the creative, intimate Trinity gave us as Covenant Lovers!

NOTES

Introduction

1. *Total Intimacy* corresponds with Lesson Six in *Covenant Lovers: God's Plan for a Celebration of Sex*, also written by Rosenau and Neel. *Covenant Lovers* is a six-session seminar with videos and workbook that explores God's intent for intimacy and sex inside the covenant of marriage. www.covenantlovers.com

Green

1. Dan Allender and Tremper Longman, *Intimate Allies,* (Wheaton, IL, Tyndale House, 1995), 11
2. John Gottman, *The Seven Principles for Making Marriage Work*, (New York: Three Rivers Press, 1999), 27-34
3. Douglas Rosenau, *A Celebration of Sex,* (Nashville: Thomas Nelson, 2002), 3
4. Aaron Beck, *Love is Never Enough,* (New York: Harper & Row, 1988), 78-79

Purple

1. Desmond Morris, *Intimate Behaviour,* (New York: Random House, 1971), abridged and used with permission.
2. Zak, Paul. *The Moral Molecule: The Source of Love and Prosperity.* Dutton Adult. 2012
3. Laurie Watson, Wanting Sex Again, (New York: Berkley Books, 2012), 141-142
4. Douglas Rosenau and Deborah Neel, *Covenant Lovers* Workbook, www.SexualWholeness.com/CASE

Orange

1. Rosemary Basson, "A Model of Women's Sexual Arousal," *Journal of Sex & Marital Therapy* 28 (2002): 17-28

2. Barry McCarthy and Emily McCarthy, *Rekindling Desire*, (New York: Brunner-Routledge, 2003), 8

3. Kathryn Hall, *Reclaiming Your Sexual Self: How You Can Bring Desire Back into Your Life*, (New York: John Wiley & Sons, Inc., 2004), 1

4. Kathryn Hall, *Reclaiming Your Sexual Self: How You Can Bring Desire Back into Your Life*, (New York: John Wiley & Sons, Inc., 2004), 82

5. Cliff and Joyce Penner, *The Way To Love Your Wife*, (Carol Stream, IL: Tyndale House, 2007), 42-43

6. Archibald Hart, Catherine Weber, and Debra Taylor, *Secrets of Eve*, (Nashville: Word Publishing, 1998), 105

7. *Shannon Ethridge, The Sexually Confident Wife*, (New York: Broadway Books, 2008), 10

8. Michael Metz and Barry McCarthy, *Enduring Desire: Your Guide to Lifelong Intimacy*, (New York: Routledge, 2011), 5

9. Michael Metz & Barry McCarthy, *Enduring Desire: Your Guide to Lifelong Intimacy*. (New York: Routledge, 2011), 16

APPENDIX

Feeling Words

How do you feel? Can you describe it? As a self-awareness exercise, use the words below to help you pin point the emotions that you are experiencing.

happy	comfortable	cheerful
up	conflicted	annoyed
hopeless	sad	elated
torn	mad	angry
furious	blocked	lonely
distressed	ecstatic	frustrated
worried	depressed	uptight
great	troubled	down
lost	discouraged	upset
excited	confused	low
hurt	nervous	envious
anxious	proud	relieved
uneasy	relaxed	pleased
stupid	vulnerable	left out
uncomfortable	disappointed	light-hearted

LOVING WITH YOUR FIVE SENSES

Download the Five Senses exercise at www.covenantlovers.com

| | *Likes* | | *Dislikes* | |
	WIFE	HUSBAND	WIFE	HUSBAND
SMELL				
SIGHT				
SOUND				
TASTE				
TOUCH				

What is a 'turn on' for you? What is a 'turn off' for you?
Combine your lists so that each of you has a complete chart.

ABOUT THE AUTHORS

Douglas E. Rosenau, Ed.D., is a Licensed Psychologist and Marriage and Family Therapist specializing in sex therapy. For the past thirty years he has maintained a private practice, acquiring skills and gaining experience while listening to over 50,000 hours of stories. Doug used this practical wisdom in authoring *A Celebration of Sex*, co-authoring *A Celebration of Sex After 50; and Soul Virgins: Redefining Single Sexuality* and a biblically based curriculum (workbook & DVD), *Covenant Lovers: God's Plan for a Celebration of Sex*. He serves as an adjunct professor at Richmont Graduate University in Atlanta, GA, Reformed Theological Seminary in Jackson, MS and at Dallas Theological Seminary.

Doug is a nationally known conference speaker and he loves to mentor and encourage. His current passion is helping to equip and empower church leaders to teach healthy sexuality within their communities as he fulfills his calling to "unveil God's truth about sexuality and cultivate a sexually health Church."

Doug jogs, reads Westerns, and loves chocolate. He and his wife Cathy have a cabin in the north Georgia mountains and enjoy being surrounded by nature. He values his friendship with his daughter Merrill and his granddaughter Caitlyn thinks Papa hung the moon.

www.dougrosenau.com
d.rosenau@sexualwholeness.com

Deborah C. Neel, Ph.D. is a Licensed Psychologist, a certified Health Services Provider – Psychologist (HSP-P) and Certified Sex Therapist (AASECT and ABCST). Early in her career she taught special education and then served as a School Psychologist with a local school system. She works closely with other healthcare providers, housing her office at one time within a pediatrician's office and most recently within an OB/GYN clinic. She has worked with children, parents, and spouses in her private practice for the past 30+ years, specializing in marital and sex therapy for the last ten. Debbie co-authored *A Celebration of Sex Guidebook* and a biblically based curriculum (workbook & DVD), *Covenant Lovers: God's Plan for a Celebration of Sex.* She speaks locally and nationally, conducting workshops, seminars and retreats on marital intimacy. Debbie helps train professional and lay people to teach God's design of healthy marital sexuality.

Debbie and her husband of 32 years, John, live in Cary, NC. Their son, Jeff and wife, Ginna, live close by with their rescue dog, Leia (princess that she is). Their daughter, Katie, with her no-longer stray cat, Lily, also lives locally. When she is not working, Debbie loves to get her fingers among her flowers. Bi-weekly trips to the local Farmers Market provides great entertainment and meals. Debbie always looks forward to Wednesday Family night dinners!

www.atriumpsychology.com
drdeb@atriumpsychology.com

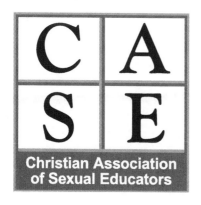

Christian Association of Sexual Educators

The Christian Association of Sexual Educators (**CASE**) desires to cultivate sexually healthy churches. As a training organization under Sexual Wholeness, Inc., CASE will equip ministry leaders to teach sexual workshops on a variety of topics within their church communities. Presently there are three workshops, directed at marriages, singles and men. Covenant Lovers is the workshop from which this Mini Book on *Total Intimacy* is developed.

"Covenant Lovers: God's Plan for A Celebration of Sex"

God placed lovers in the amazing, stretching covenant of marriage. Fantastic marital lovemaking is built on the foundation of God-reflective sexuality, effective communication skills, a healthy understanding of masculine and feminine gender differences, and three key colors of total intimacy.

"Dance of the Sexes: Celebrating the Soul in Single Sexuality"

"Singles are sexually whole" as they demonstrate a different but equally important aspect of God's sexual plan: enjoying masculinity and femininity created in His image, celebrating the fun interaction and complementarity of men and women, valuing a 3-dimensional (body, mind, spirit) social and erotic sexuality.

"God's Heroes and Warriors: Becoming Men of Sexual Integrity and Influence"

Three critical Strategies help men: Accept Their Sexual Significance, Fight for Sexual Integrity and Grow into Sexual Influence. Godly men find their true masculinity, enjoy and discipline sexual desire, fight Satan's sexual distortions, "knight up" for the women in their lives as they follow Jesus, their True North and God's sexual strategies.

For more information go to **SexualWholeness.com** and click on the CASE icon.

"Covenant Lovers: God's Plan for A Celebration of Sex"

In a practical, engaging and informative way, this workshop develops six crucial areas for cultivating deeper sexual intimacy in marriage. This Mini Book was taken from the sixth lesson of this workbook's material. The six lessons in this course help marital partners and Covenant Lovers to:

☐ Apply God-reflective sexuality (creatively intimate, mysteriously beautiful, passionately present, and intentionally holy) to enrich their lovemaking in their incredible covenant of marriage.

☐ Incorporate effective sexual communication skills that can enhance a love life with better initiating and declining interactions, heal the past, and stir up passion by creating dialogue before, during and after lovemaking.

☐ Understand and integrate a healthy understanding of masculinity and femininity, while they make the most of those gender differences and learn how to apply the accelerators and avoid the brakes to a great sex life.

☐ Explore the importance of those crucial erogenous zones with an understanding of sexual arousal, and utilize natural aphrodisiacs to expand their love life.

☐ Incorporate a color-coded model for deepening total intimacy in their marriage, from the bonding Green of intimate companions, to the coupling purple of sensuous lovers, and the igniting Orange of erotic playmates.

For more information on Covenant Lovers workshops go to **SexualWholeness.com** and click on the CASE icon, or go to **www.covenantlovers.com**.

Made in the USA
Charleston, SC
24 April 2016